Liminal Women

A Drink from the Wellspring

ISBN: 979-8-218-29220-1

Table of Contents

Jennifer Goldring

Editor's Note

One pre-pandemic spring day, three women who had recently turned 40 sat on a patio and talked about their next forty years. These women came from a variety of backgrounds; they had been divorced, two had teenagers, they'd all changed careers, gone back to school, gotten their master's degrees in various disciplines, and decided they were going to make the next 40 years the best years of their lives. It's a little hard to come to terms with entering mid-life, but that's where we were: three women entering mid-life and feeling finally ready to take on the world.

We talked about how to do that. This time in our lives felt liminal, like we were on the cusp of something unfamiliar, wonderful, and promising. We talked about how knowing yourself better and being more accepting of your flaws, failures, successes, and disappointments could allow you to fully understand yourself. We all agreed we were nearly fully there. And that is how this anthology, Liminal Women: A Drink from the Wellspring, was born. After more discussion, we thought it would be wonderful to give other women a voice and a place to share the same feeling of being liminal and being on the precipice of something, whatever and however that manifested for them.

As we read submissions, it became apparent that each submitter experienced their share of trauma, love, and becoming. To us, that feels like part of the essence of being a woman. It may sound sad, but that is how we've been treated by society, family, and loved ones, often as if we are disposable, useless, or ruined. One thing writing has given to all of us is a platform and a voice to share all these feelings and a path back to who we truly are when we've been lost. Writing is the thing that allows us to relate with one another and to know we are truly not alone, truly not unlovable, truly not disposable, and truly deserving of having our voices elevated. We represent a small slice of humanity and are a reminder that women are powerful, pioneering, and resilient no matter what liminal place we may be in. Not only do all the women who shared their work with us deserve to be read, seen, and heard, but they must be!

A last thought: this anthology has been a true labor of love, and all the people involved have had the patience of saints, especially our contributors! We genuinely appreciate your sticking with us and helping this anthology become a reality! Sending all of you so much love for the women you were when this project began and the women you have become and will become as time passes. ☙

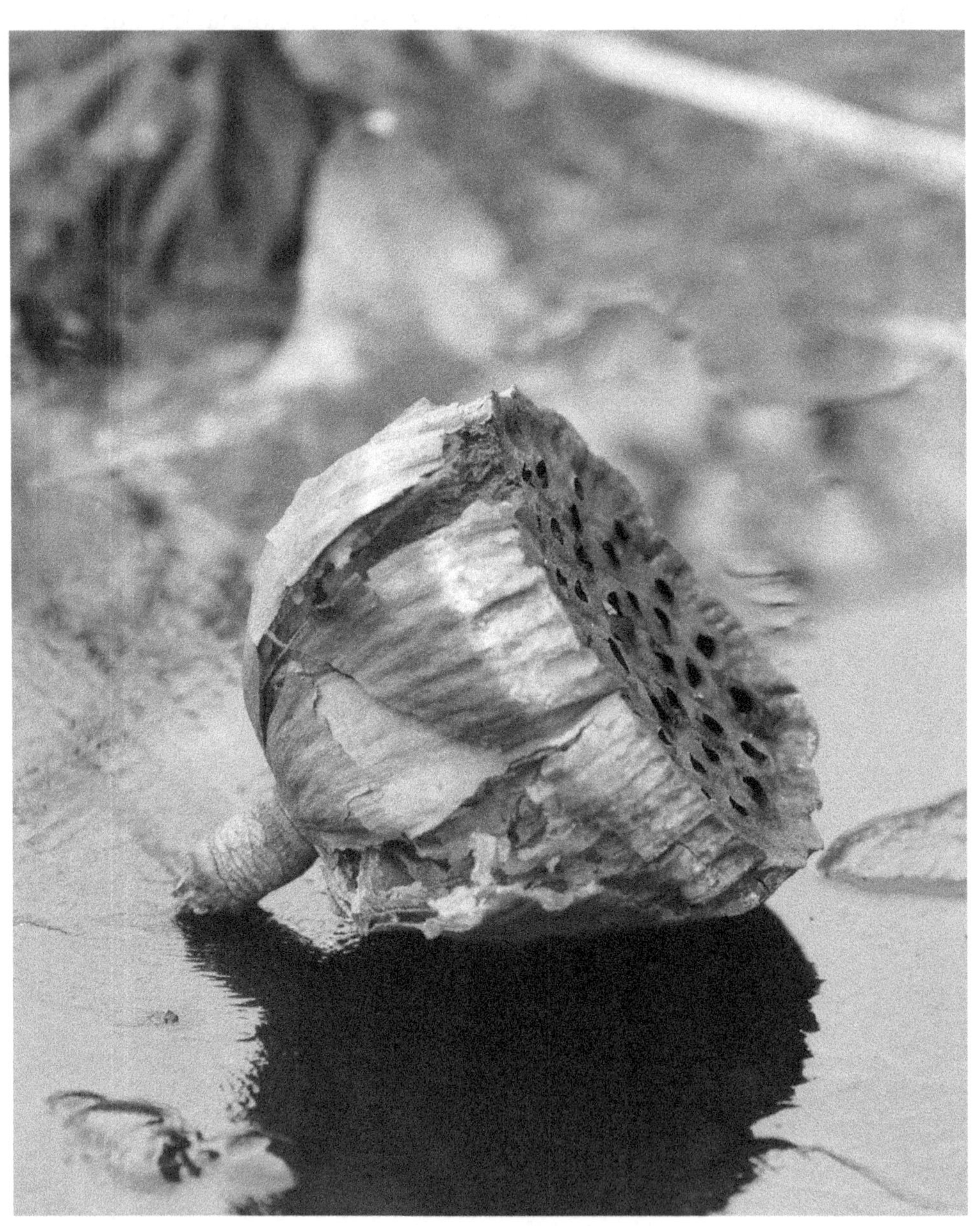

Jennifer Goldring
Some New Beginning (2020)

Kelli Allen

All I can see burning, and no reflection

Robberies are often quiet.
Our hands are in the air
while we sleep and the silo
empties twenty grains
at a time. When the chamber
echoes a hungry belly,
we pay attention only
to how deep our cups, how thin
our woven mats and cricket
high grass. I wonder

at nobility. There are four crowns
for taking, sacks open over
the well's lip. Remember
when everything after
the saddle meant asking
to be wanted? You, too, are Tiresias—
the staff you hold burns figs
as they leave branches to baptize
some sand too long in the sun.

* Previously published in *Blue Mountain Review*, &
the collection *Banjo's Inside Coyote* by Kelli Allen

Jeanne Allison

Two Pictures From My Mother's Life

I listen to the muffled call of the neighborhood night owl as I sit
on the screened-in porch, pondering images from my mother's life,

faint in family memories: A baby—screaming in a basket
in a scorching cotton field of silence as terror ripped a young mother's heart—

a brother my mother never knew, the heat too much for his body.
Grandma never forgave herself for caving to the judging murmurs

of other women in camp when there was no choice
but to pick cotton with the baby at her feet. And a sister—

an aunt I never knew—calling my mother hot- shit-on-a-stick
because of her fierce way, forcing them to pay attention,

even the brothers getting ready for war. And Grandma's indulgence
of her tenth child—my mother—a surprise, supposedly dead

already after yet two more children died of a fever—one just before Thanksgiving
and the other just after Christmas. But the stillbirth never happened,

my mother's body tiny as a hand, a bright screaming light emerging
from a long and unholy night. That owl has outlived my mother now,

high in the sky at dusk as a cathedral of trees shifts in the breeze
over a gravesite chosen for the beauty of Dogwoods in bloom.

Lani Arness

Cresting Wave

There is always a beginning.
We'll call her Eve,
a disturbance, a blue wave
curve of bone and breath.

There is always an end,
a falling apart,
chaotic diffusion of particles
that cry out and never leave.

Eve—swaying movement
of hip and rib—a sudden disruption.
(Just before the sun exhales, you see her,
blue water, rising.)

Nature is so mathematical.
You can measure the length
from one rise to the next and find patterns
repeating—begin and end.

Eve in undulation.
She arches the small of her back,
curves her fingers around the apple,
bites in.

The sun rises on a garden—empty.
Eve, who will speak to the snakes every time,
sings, rolls stones across a barren field.
She is rising.

Maria F. Balogh

UNRULY

At four the girl
ran her fingers
through her aunt's
          straight hair
                    unlike her own
so admirable & appealing
not to find knots
as she smoothed
several strands at a time
                    transfixed

At six the girl sat patiently
on grandma's lap as the woman
untangling the girl's hair
made futile attempts
to shield her granddaughter
from thoughtless remarks
of a neighbor
   a friend of the family
                  a great aunt

Tame that pelo malo
          Use this new lotion
There is a new brand
                    of combing conditioner
that could relax that big mess

At 15 the girl
a slave to the straightening iron
the leave in creams

the net she wears
every two nights
to keep the *vuelta*
that allows her to have
"good" hair for a few days
dismisses the compliments
her 13-year-old cousin
now receives after freeing
her own "bad" hair of irons
& brushes & tamers & nets
who parades a voluptuous head
of black curls
          proudly liberated

Rebecca Kiwi Barnstien

Mother Shaped Hole

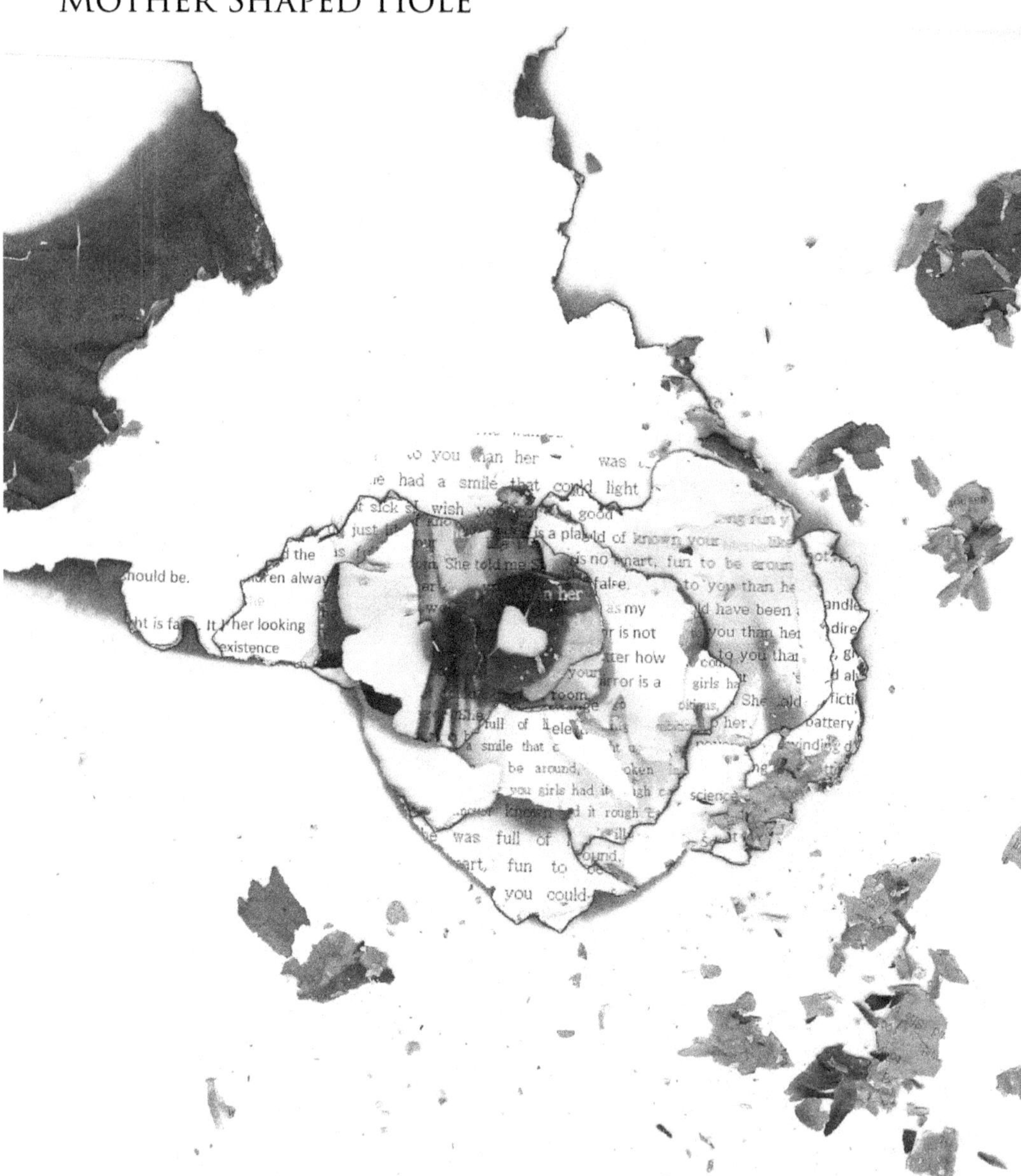

I bought an electric candle, which flickered and had a five-hour timer. It fit in my hand. As I thought of my mother, I set the candle on fire. The batteries leaked acid, and it smelled terrible. I was surprised at how well the candle burned. Look at you, you little liar, look at you burn, but you don't even do that right, it's all toxic smoke and smoldering wires.

. I know you girls h
e wanted to be a better
ng is could of known your mom lik
he would have been a good
smart, fun to be around, out spoken.
mart fun to be around, o spoken.
ne than her can as to
gift of destruction?

you than her was
had a smile that could light up
oom. I wish you could of known your
Mother
like I did. I see all of that in you.
She had a smile that could light up a
room. In the long run you girls grew up
ust like she did. She told me Sh
wanted to be a better to you than
her was to her. I wish you could o
known your She like I did. She told m
She wanted to be a better to yo
than her was to her. I wish yo
could of known your She is she is like I did.
wish you could of known your li
did. She was full of life, outgoi
mbitious, smart, fun to be arou
tspoken. I wish you could of
like I did. mother

should be.

light is false. It leads me in
I remember
white, screaming
sad, but no matter how sad
This flickering is an illusion
taking me with her.
creation? I have a candle that is
like a candle but it never has
light, but there is no heat.

I am fire

was not what she

is an electric candle, the
wrong direction
in the color blue, ghost
us beautiful and always
it is a fiction, a
battery trick
winding down,
hitting rock bottom and
White is the gift of
not a candle, which looks
that waxy smell. It casts a
am I, with false

?

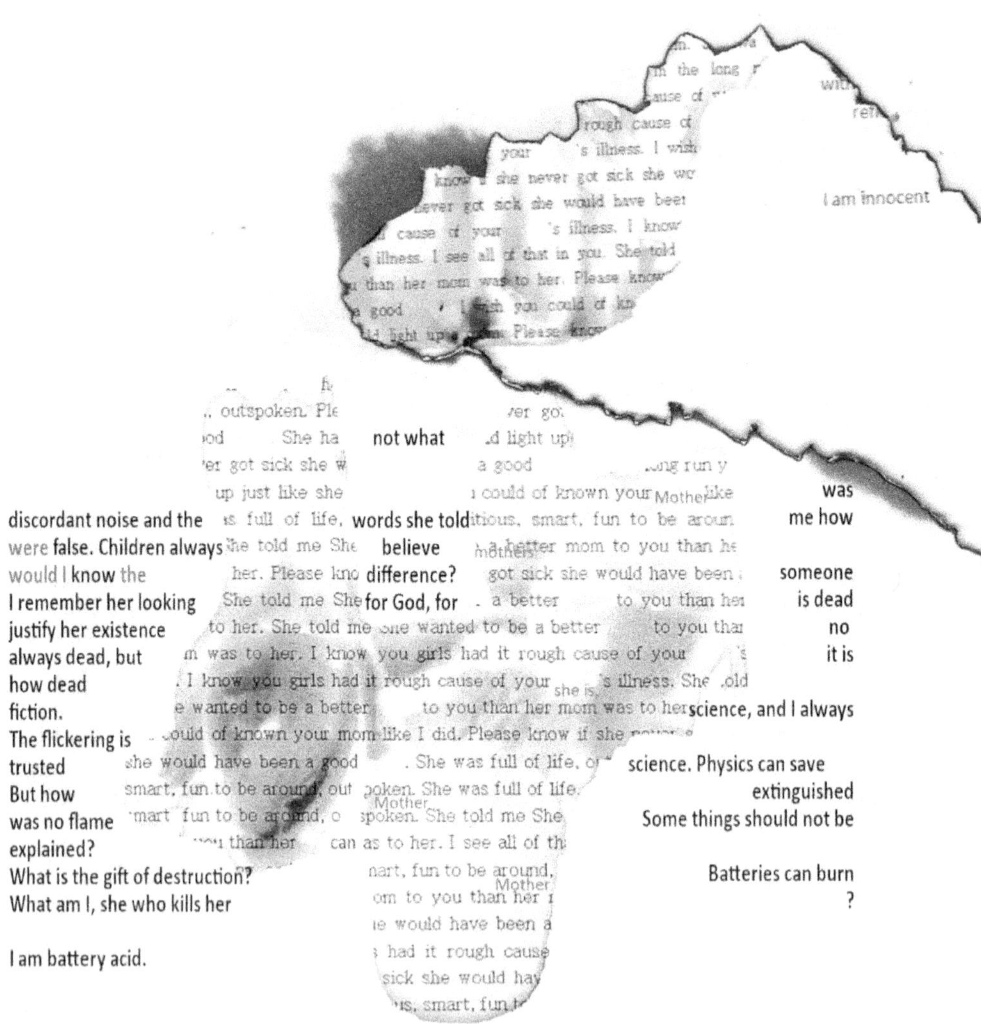

I am innocent

not what

was

discordant noise and the words she told me how

were false. Children always believe

would I know the difference? someone

I remember her looking for God, for is dead

justify her existence no

always dead, but it is

how dead

fiction. science, and I always

The flickering is

trusted science. Physics can save

But how extinguished

was no flame Some things should not be

explained?

What is the gift of destruction? Batteries can burn

What am I, she who kills her ?

I am battery acid.

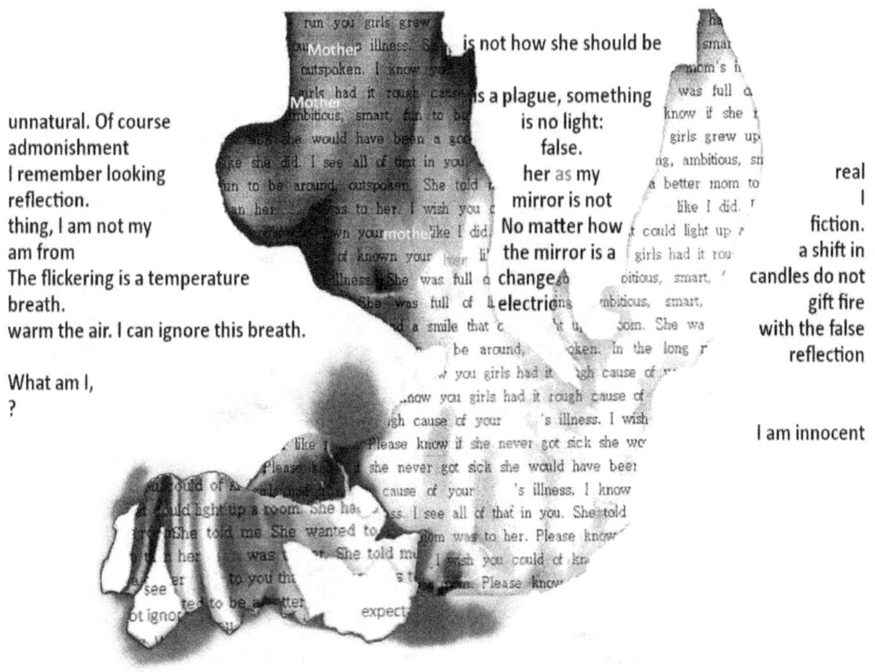
Mother
is not how she should be
Mother
is a plague, something
unnatural. Of course
is no light:
admonishment
false.
I remember looking
her as my
reflection.
mirror is not
thing, I am not my
mother
No matter how
am from
the mirror is a
The flickering is a temperature
change
breath.
electric
warm the air. I can ignore this breath.
real
I
fiction.
a shift in
candles do not
gift fire
with the false
reflection
What am I,
?
I am innocent

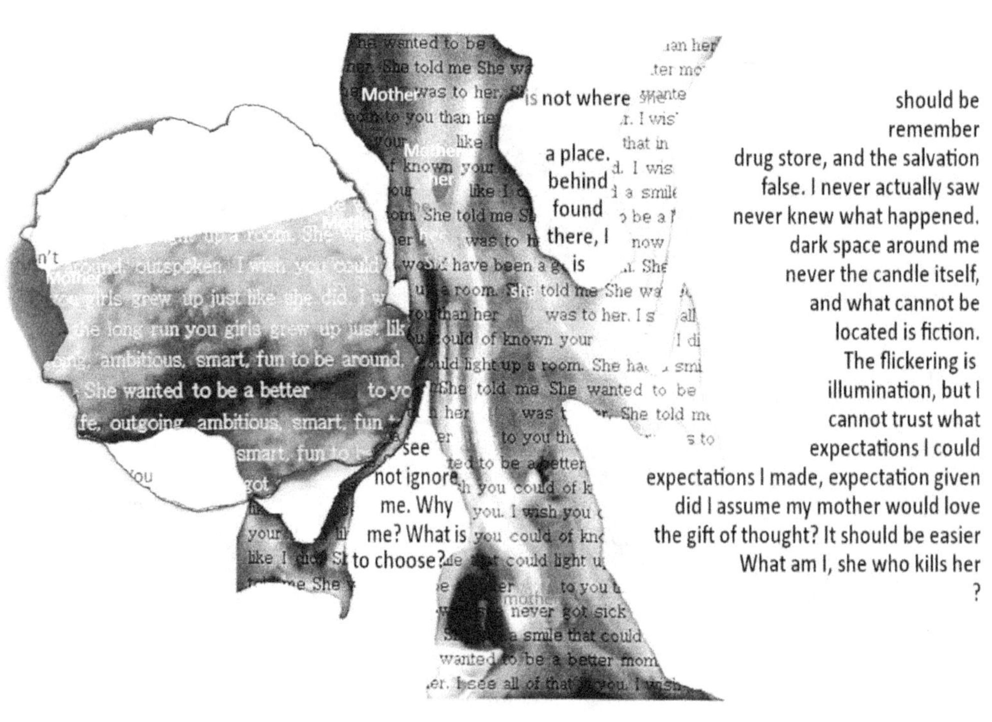

I am honey red vengeance.

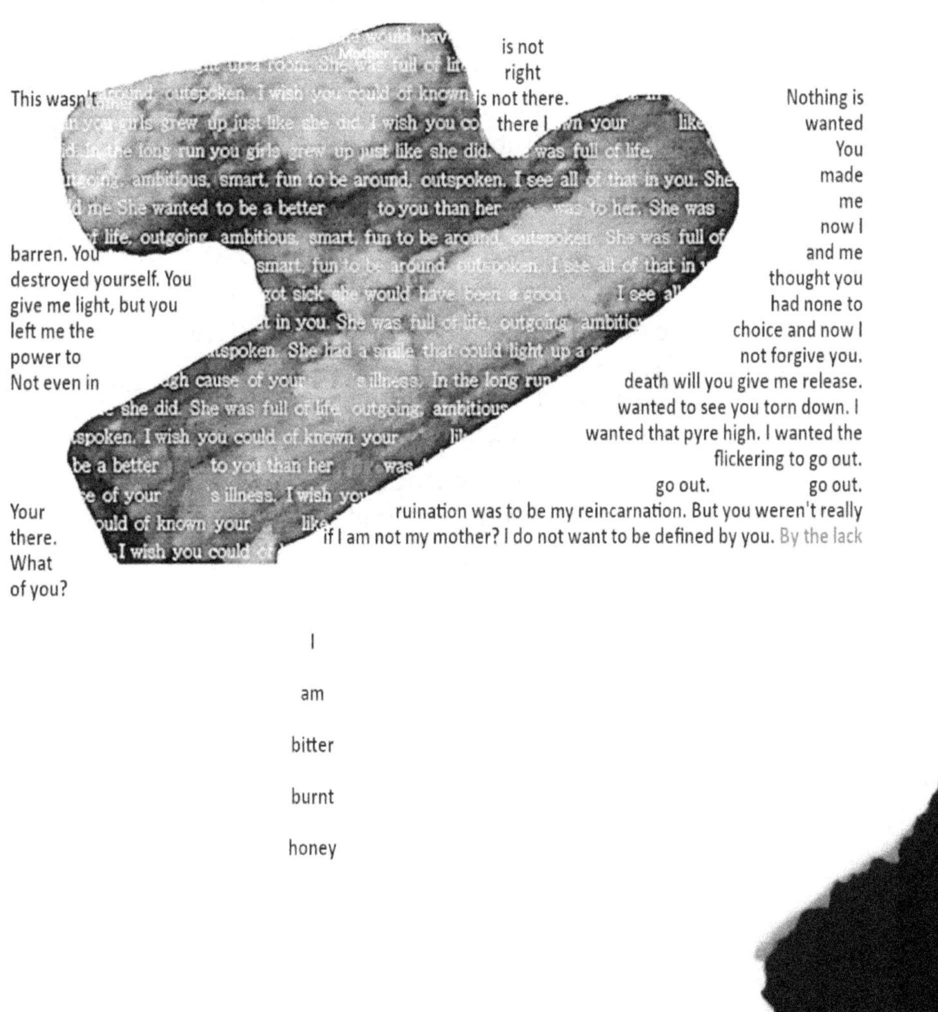

I

am

bitter

burnt

honey

Lauren Beck

KNOWING

we are from the bluff hills of Missoura
from muddy murky river roads.

we are from flowing, flooding waters
surging, slicing through the land
clay earth clinging to sturdy hands

i came from fallow fields
falling timber, growing steel

Earth-bounded bindings
borders, boundaries

we are of inner strength and outward stone
of ripened love and life's compassion
we are from the fragile, leathered hands
In rhythmic procession
warshing clothes,
holding, folding
Rising up
reuniting

Michelle Chen

If You Never Learn Religion It Becomes Vestigial

Siren of the body / ballad to travel / higher powers were uninteresting / for your parents / for your lightness / love the muck / and the sky / an interesting wind / radioactivity / shook something loose / in you your gallery / of bones reaches joy / the same and cake / can be eaten / without the / appendix / blood is / in your nose / and not / ribbon soft / not staked / if while reading these words you slip into prayer / unheard / and wide river county brings you / pride / through canyons / the slit doze of roadkill / absolute in its girth / and the introvert / speaking into silence / hears only peace / if you cannot change angels from baubles to cloud-chasers / the coccyx is a fused tail that formed when we rose / one day you don't know whether you want a God or more friends / the hair lifting off our bodies / as if on fire / the feet flat like in a painting / an autopsy / if no listener could be better than the air you breathe / the beautiful organs / across your body like fruit / warm you / mysteriously / small curled mammals / content / on your chest the need not there / for a deity / to ask for some eating through you / of inheritance / if you sometimes do wonder / if the apple was sweet / and the hand full of water / the old meat and white trunk good / for balance and rawness / see your body in a snake's / joyous flicker / you lay your head down for sleep / not slumber

At the Naval Home

Sun hits between her shoulders a harpoon
amid whalebones, and she mists sunscreen
onto the burnt back of her neck, excess oil pooling
in freckles on the white walk.
My mother pulls the rope in my chest
in her fisherman way, hauling
a basket of crabs – spray, seep, sway, blister.
Down at the mirror little boats draw lace chisels
on the sea, who is indecisive (up, down, goose, whale).
The visitor center is a blind-white, façade the white-curved
back of a cornea. In its gut are little model ships,
an old spacesuit, air conditioning. Then we're out again
on veteran's lane where American flags are folded
into large carnations then hung on every house.
Black cannons like the muzzles of dogs
brush, here and there, my mother's hand.
On the museum steps there's a black anchor
whose insides sizzle in the sun.
She rubs them – hands to warm them up,
toes just-dipped in Annapolis to dry.
The cemetery curls its thick tail around the map.
A fox's russet, its bushiness prunes imps from our oxygen
and its animal ruff nips open the world like a boiled mollusk.
We're smiling, our hands are cold. *Don't*
think you'd fit in, my mother says, our displacement
rustling sails, teasing some fog out of the folds.
Course not, but I'd like some strength
to lead her back across the ocean.
To craft with calluses a cat's cradle
to this place until someday I become
midshipman, souvenir. When I can say *home*
to the tall joggers pulling flesh and small fish
above chin-up bars, warm a house on my stomach
and carry it wherever I go.
Her baleen hands gather krill, sweat.
Mint leaves grow from the corners of our mouths.

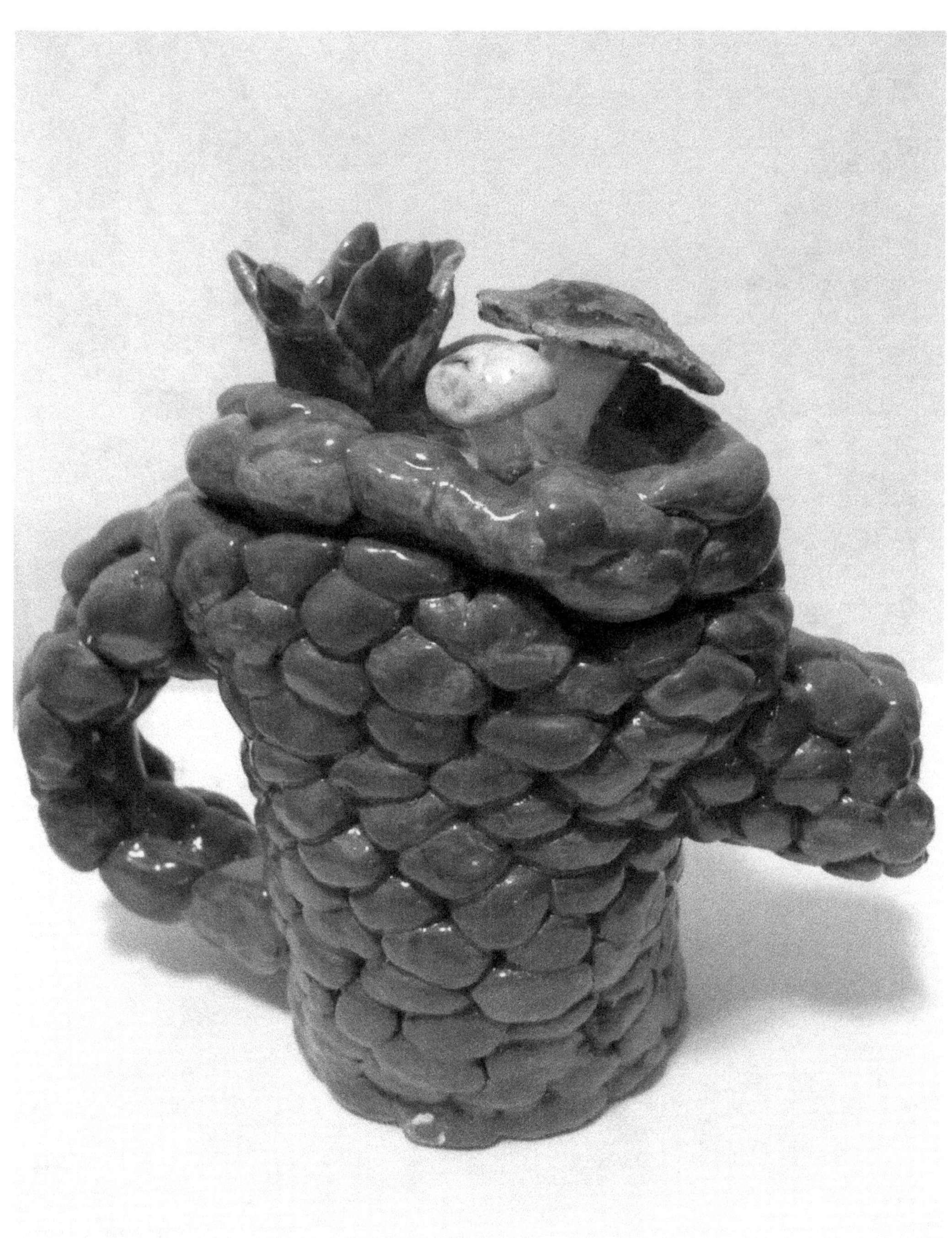

Michelle Chen
Time of the Month

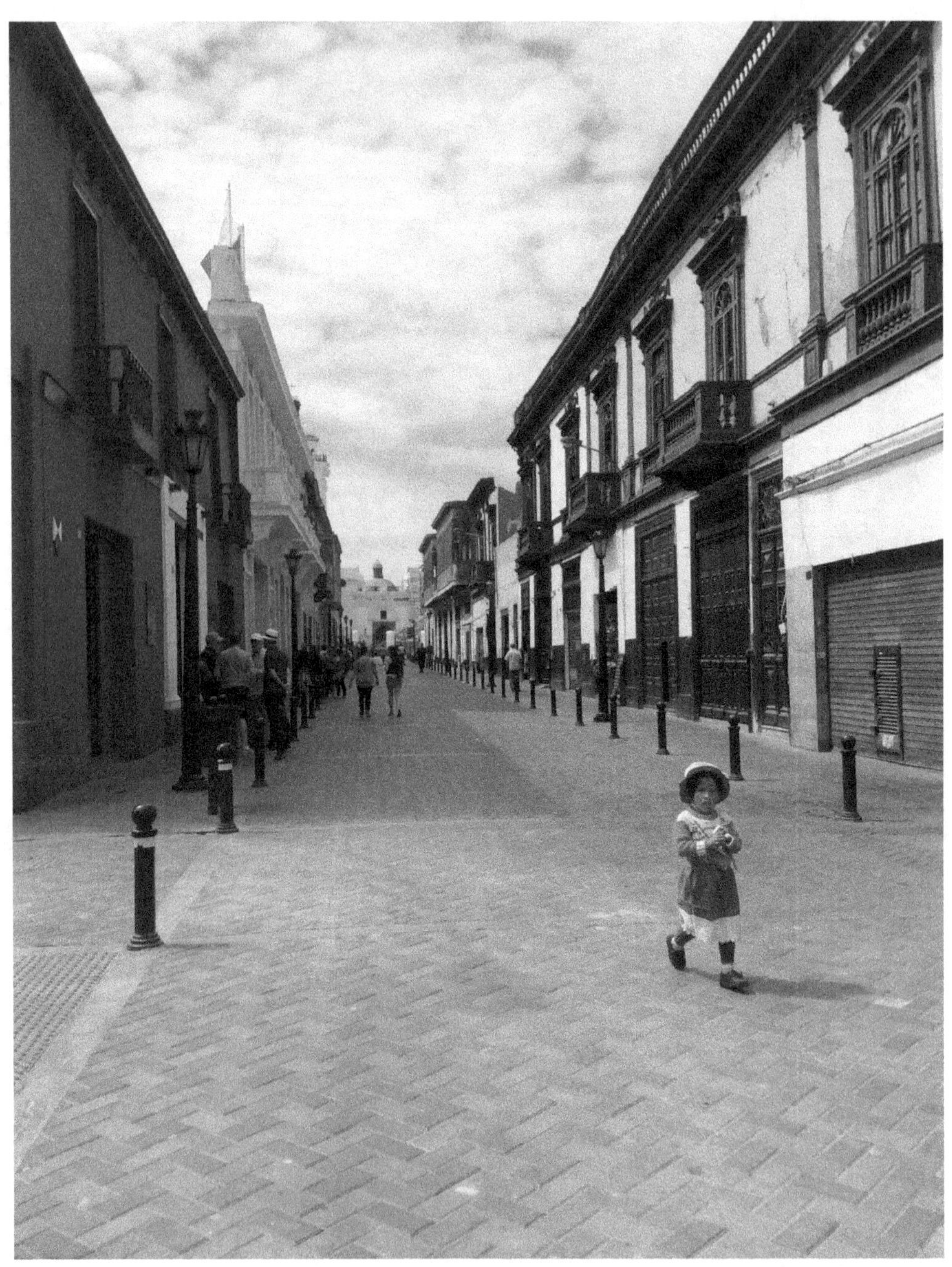

Michelle Chen
Red (Lima)

Dawn Dupler

Processions

My mother cleaves herself to me before we enter the room. Organ music parts a sea of chairs, one heavy step from one hunched body, onlookers stealing our air. God, how I resent their here-now, there-now presence. *It's not him,* I say but her red plum face faces forward and her tears shriek but their colors are under water and again I say, *It's not him.* So much and so little preparation for this walk and at its end stands a preacher next to my beige father, lying at me from a box. Lined lips, rouge-thick, she smiles then pushes me but I am white-gown-heavy. Others stand against gravity's pull. God, how I resent their, his, your, my presents hiding in a corner. The first preacher pinned the lid years ago and now a fresh peach opens a book next to a man in a tuxedo. At the end of this new walk, both smile at me and iron-rust tears drown all sound but this: *It's not him.*

Renee Emerson

ROCKABYE

Seesaw, Swaying Bridge,
your every move is contingent on his,
a counterbalance to the idiot
steps of his drunkenness.

You'll call this *chess* or *tango*
but let's call it what it is:
a leash, tether, gravitational
pull. Mother, remember

how he tells the story
of sleeping propped against
the wall, holding me as a baby,
maybe, unsure if I were
phantom or firstborn?

I used to love that
story, the moon's sort
of sacrifice, keeping watch
through the night.
Until I became a mother,
held my own infant asleep
in my arms and thought if
the baby should fall,
what a solid, final
sound it would make.

Jill Evans

On Leaving Home

It takes forever. And still
you never get there.
It is a destination, this
leave-taking,
a deep sky you cross under
beneath the unknown.

It is an intractable breath
echoing your first newborn cry
or the willowy sigh of a spring storm
in the wide open changes
of everything,
when your mother and father are busy,
their eyes turned away. You go on
beginning.

You take with you
all you can bear:
your reputation,
your old habits,
all your unease heaped inside you
like old unfolded clothes. You stockpile
miscellaneous flatteries, back-up plans
for an understudy to love you,
other maps of the self.

You bring caution with you
like a compass. You carry
your old opinions held rigid
as unbending postures
tensed against the wind.

You hoard sugary daydreams entwined
in the sheerest garments of time.
You send out flares
made of shiny words. Like these.

And you wonder if
you will fall from far away.
And just who
you will turn into
when you do.

*Previously published – *Prime Circle Press*, Canada, March, 2020

THE SURVIVOR'S PEP TALK

I told her it gives us endless dreams:
this malignancy
this slow disease
we each must live with now
a frantic grief, I said
like nesting dolls of diagnostic words
cramming all the fears
into a nightmare
into a blur

a foreign language for ourselves
for the self we have not yet become:
that very one
we can't imagine
the one we might easily have gone on being
so simple, so unique
taking time discovering
just who we might want to be
inside the only body we will have

and for the other, wiser
might-have-beens
still unknown
to that final, finished self

only yesterday
when we were still becoming:
that same superstitious person,
within our body's nightmares
swollen in our sleep

– and so this sickness
gives us salty patience
to learn better
how to falter
how to make a fetish
of our ticking breath:

the time it takes –
and takes away and
somehow still
we dream

so we can:
find the taste of
our own tongues again
even in the flow
of wine winding down a glass
even in the laughter about the ever-after
that sparks up now and then
and still

She is learning just how much
hope we dare
dole out
for our own
uncertain selves.

I told my friend:
it makes us stronger.

Beverly Fesharaki

UNSTRANGLED

The object of this poem is to free
us from strangled spiritual growth,
rescue us from the lake of the afraid.

There are no requirements,
no book littered with rules,

You might
lurch forward into the fragrance
of lavender,
let a cedar-wood branch guide
you to a god you can touch,

or rest like Joni Mitchell
in the grateful climate of song.

I'll meet you there.

A Taste of Silence

Then and there I made room for sadness.
Crows cawing in the trees,

bird voices—a warning.
The motor boats full throttle,

they sound too—rumble, "I'm
coming," as you loudly announce

the silence in your leaving,
the absence of your noise.

Unrippled water in your wake,
warm here and now.
I was never sorry.

Michelle Lizet Flores

My Abuela Was a Seamstress

In memory of the Triangle Shirtwaist Factory Fire of 1911

She sewed many things:
bathing suits, dresses, jackets, buttons.

She too found place in the New York sweatshops
trading fabrica for factoria,
lavandería for laundri,
El Oriente for Brooklyn.

These women.
Their work.

The chains on each door.
The thread in each bobbin.
The prick of each needle.

Did their nietas wonder
why they didn't make it home
for dinner that night?

Were their lovers waiting
underneath a marquee?

These women
flinging themselves
out of windows,

their blood runs
in the air
in me.

* previously published in *Azahares*, UAFS' Spanish-Language literary magazine

Jessica Freeman
On Clark Street

On Clark Street and Berwyn
I tended the bar
and danced on tables when they asked me—
I had no back up plan
no relative to call home for money.
I listened when the owner told me
to open the top button
of my black tuxedo shirt
then the next,
then the next,
then the next,
until the crest of my breast
appeared under the little bit of coke
still stuck to the top of his mustache.
And when he brought his best friend from the suburbs
they sidled up
to where I lit candles
prepped lemons, limes, basil and oranges,
filled sugars sets,
my chapped hands rolling
cheap silverware before service,
and they stood behind me with bloated red faces
under the *Family Establishment* sign
asking if rent was due
before dropping sweaty fifties
in my apron pocket
next to pita triangles and cheese wedges
I'd stolen to take home.
And when I left my station to go the bathroom
they followed, trying to jam me
up against the wall in the fluorescent hallway
murmuring how good I sliced through the fruit
how that short apron accented my pointy hips.
And they asked if I wanted some grappa
to start the night off right

before I could slam the bathroom door
in a blur of mangy faces
and the owner winked,
Remember, pull your apron strings tight.
I took those crinkled fifties
and didn't say a word
because I was a crater-sized scar
and every one of those bars was the same
with coke, spandex aprons,
men in fluorescent hallways.
I came back because the bursar kept kicking me
out of class for unpaid bills
and my brother needed medicine
and nothing was ever going to be enough.
So, I stayed and stayed and stayed
until words and beliefs became mean-nothing
fragments crawling outside of me
swimming around incandescent light.
I took that cash home
sat in my own season of rot
and suffocation at the pink and gold table
in my studio next to the Jarvis el stop
where fat icicles bled down my windows
and I counted every dollar twice
ordered bills across the table like his coke lines,
and hid it all in my rent can
before opening a beer
and running to the bathroom
to let fly his sickness
I was washed in.

River Street Greenhouse: Kalamazoo, Michigan

In late February I work the assembly line
from dark until dark,
and I wait for light that never arrives
in this place where winter widens inside of me.

I had wanted to feel my fingers dig under soil
to take my body to land

mold roots, anchor into beauty
make *something.*

Instead, I stand in cold water at the conveyor belt
with hipsters and laid off auto workers
shoving labels over plastic grooves
on containers of dill, caraway, lemon balm.

I drive pallets down Market Street to L Street to River,
wheels slide over layers of unimaginably thick ice
which somehow remind me of cow udders ready to burst;
gas fumes choke me at the wheel.

Here I don't talk in the language of the living.

At night I dream about kudzu and pulchella flowers,
pink and purple seeds turned to silk bright stars
bursting from ice, set free
from synthetic soil and plastic pots.

Neither the plants nor I are at home here.
I can imagine the herbs neither living
nor dying, nor turning toward sun.
They are objects, just *things* for show.

Jennifer Goldring
House of Wrens

full of   becoming
    softness   and light
        full of chittering
that can't be   quelled
calls
        that won't be
                silenced
little nest   of need
        and want
mouths open
            and singing
      notes to fill this silence
resonante and ring
                but don't tire
        the tympanic nerve
a necessary message

welcome to this house
        of mouth full of song
house of a modicum
                of humility
   this house
        of love   house
                of love
this house — full to
                overflowing —
        of wrens

Abigail for Green

House Split by LIght

Recovery looks like light that hums
on a hot summer day when the air is electric
and the molecules that make up the chair I sit on, Jennifer,
begin to vibrate
and I have the sense that nothing is holding me
that the chair is a song and it is vibrating I wonder how
anything is held together
I don't know it's hard to say but I want you to know
that it is happening
take note of my new address: House Split by Light
I hope you can find it
please come

Liberty Heise

My Splendid Catch

for C.D.

is not the size of a hand
but is the size of shards flung in natural patterns
left by ear-ache winds
through photographs of my farming ancestors.
From the cardboard box I pull
the white edged photograph of
grandmother,
having not always been a grandmother,
she is sitting in a field
not far from the farmhouse kitchen I am currently in.
Her rich, black hair is caught in motion -
free of pins or bonnet.
Her dress is flipping itself upward,
her smile, cutting through the drift of smoke
produced by the rolled cigarette
in her familiar hand.
From the same box,
jumping back a generation before,
I find a booklet, hand-made.
My great-grandmother's notes on her preferences
for the farm-hood boys who have given her
their pictures.
My dad leans in to say,
she was once a real heart-breaker.
My great-grandfather has a cameo in the booklet
a white heart is drawn around his head.
I hear her, in the dry and edgy tone her
unsmiling farm life had crafted, say,
"he'll have to do."

* previously published in *Scintilla* at scintillapress.com

Nasheetah Hossain

Wanderess Part 2
Colors

I lay there in a white dress under the 5 am sky. The cold black hue of the sky was indomitable when I got here.

I was at that point, trying to figure myself out, caging parts of me in categories of conflicting vocabulary. I could never just be one single person. I don't think adjectives could ever illustrate me. Colours. I could think of colors.

Green is grotesque to me. Yellow is too merry, black too dull. I'm too unadorned to be golden, too subtle to be red too bold to be blue. I bury my face in my pillows. This is overbearing.

The first flare of the sun slices through the darkness, so golden it could be white. The black pigment condenses into the clouds as they turn pastel. Bursts of pink and purple splatter across. The stars start to blink softly before they die away, like the breaths of a shot bird before it expires. And the dew on the leaves are filled with gold before they droop slowly over the edges and fall to the ground.

With all these colors right before my eyes, the answer comes to me in waves. I don't think I'm supposed to be any of them. I think, I'm nothing but a plain white canvas.

Take the colors out of the sky, right after the sun rises, and paint on me. With every stroke, let pain slit through me if it means I can be something. Let the artwork of the society infiltrate through me in forms of injustice and misconceptions if it means I will gain experience. Let me open my eyes, let me out of this void. I am yet to become.

Wandress Part 4
Illicit

Evanescent,
I was the clogged breath in your throat

Cynosure,
Though I am the breath that fogged your vision.

Ineffable,
I can't show you what I am

Denouement,
Was trying to comprehend how I function.

Words,
I was poetry
Something that had one too many ways to be inferred.

Red,
You watch me unblinkingly
Late at night
Right at sunrise
Till your eyes go red.
And when you find me
It'd be like an epiphany
And when you touch me
It'll feel daringly illicit
And I'll smile and say
Tag, you're it.

Anastasia Jill

CURRENT

I understand little
but in my world

girls are made of wires
and girls who love girls can be made
Of anything;

Mostly indentations,
question marks tattooed on skin
stretching new capacities
formed from beauty.

there is a form of electricity,
the zigzag of waves that spell
out that girls are basically pacemakers –

steady and firm,
skipping hears like some
skip rope – if life is arrhythmia,

she is treatment for the globe.

Crystal Vaults

I plug my fingers into the back of a power box
While she charges her spirit on angelite.

I am power, she is soul;
We build a church; I make her a lit altar.

There are many truths for her lips to speak
To me.

Debbie Koetje Kelly

Prayer at the Confluence of Current River and Sinking Creek

Joe was going to fish and shoot pictures
find words in the holy images of stones, stems, stream
what he does
how he heals

I want to walk upstream and float down
Walk upstream, float down
walk upstream, float down to
daughter of the divine
sister of the stream
no one's wife
no one's mother
young
held
buoyed
carried
part of the sparkling water on top

I do not want to look at my son on the shore.
I do not want to see him too clearly.
For a few moments I don't want to see him at all.

I am pleading up the river
pleading down
pleading up
pleading down
I just want to see the water.
Please.

I don't want to see him on every shore we've ever found.
Sitting.
Throwing stones.
For almost three decades.

Sitting.
Throwing stones.
Watching the water.
I don't want to see all the ways he's kept on shore, watching the water.
I do not want to see how weak his left side has been since he was two; how he can't trust it in a moving stream.
I do not want to see his right hand too crumpled to hold a fishing pole or skip a rock
I do not want to see the tremors keeping him from learning photography with his dad.
I don't need to see how my son is stuck on the shore and is not in the stream.

I see that every day.
Today I pray for peace.

The currents keep pulling me back to him;
To Tom, my son.

I join him.

You've been throwing stones in water since the first time at Sam Baker Park when you were two.
Remember, you were Yoda, I was Leia, and Jud was Han.
You loved it since then.

He nods with his serene smile.

Lake Michigan
Dunn Lake
Lake Superior
Watch Hill
Huzzah Creek
St. Francois
Missouri
Mississippi
Logan Creek
This spot more times than I can count.

What do you like about it?

He describes and demonstrates
all the different sounds and splashes he can create
choosing different sizes
changing the number he throws
determining the depth of the landing place.
He creates a symphony
          Using stones, stream, strokes.

I am sitting next to Buddha in the body of my son.

He encourages me to side hand toss a hand full of the smallest pebbles.
He knows it is the sound I will love most.
I do.

What do you like best about this?

It always turns turquoise.

It does? No matter what?

Always.

Always?

Always.

Joe shoots pictures of the sunlit turquoise splashes
As we throw stones in the middle of the stream
where Sinking Creek meets the Current River

Options When Facing A Familiar Terror

Freeze
Fake calm
Curse
Call the doctor
Trust the nurse
Give the medicine
Laugh at old movies
Hold the dogs
Pick a fight
Call a friend
Crochet a shawl
Devour sweets
Stare
Try to breathe
Stop thinking
Pray
Hold on
Find the poem

Belinda Kremer

POEM FOR TAHITIA

for Tahitia Keoualani Kremer 31 March 1940—24 January 2015

Descending Mount Wittenberg trail, New Year's Eve, chilly, just before sunset.
A half hour before, at the top of Mount Wittenberg,
picking out the shapes of Drake's Estero
shifting into alien dusky landscapes of light, fog, and air.
The last of the warmth
in the last of the sun
on the last day of the year;
then the sunlight casting its long shadow of shade
across the pines ridging Sky Trail, and time to head down to Bear Valley—

  and some birds silent, and some birds calling, flew

  the light at Tomales echoing from Limantour

—I thought of you,
and how I'll never spell your name for a stranger again:

T a h i t i a

Tahitia
"Like the island," we would say,
"But soft, and with an 'a.'"

Orion

Later, driving the quiet dark
on narrow Hwy 37, Vallejo to Suisun
I watch Orion

He is setting, or rising
  —he looks like he is falling,
so low is he to the horizon, suspended parallel
over the black velvet pincushions
that flash slowly the red the naval lights of Suisun.

Phone Booth

Three days off the ferry to Alaska, a month out of college, two days into a summer of dish wash and waiting dawn tables Denali's Jewelbox. Early one night, the northern sun full bright, I begin a rambling climb, an hour later to lose my grip on a high cliff of shale and schist, the rock sheering off in my hands

—a long scrabbling drop, a ledge to smash a cheekbone on the way down, an ankle shattered; the luck of another kid out for a ramble; ambulance to the ranger station and a surgeon called in who sets me and stitches my face...

In a haze of painkillers, back at the park, I call my mother from an indoor phone booth between the restaurant's hostess station and its bar, to say I've fallen and my face and ankle are broken but I'm okay—

only I pass out in the booth, the phone cord dangling, my mother calling my name. I come to to kind strangers and a manager saying my mother is waiting, and can I talk to her, and I can hear her
—"Are you there?"—
and how I have frightened her, but can say Yes, I am here

—and I think of all of the other phone booths,
all of the times I dialed my mother from a faraway place
to share a small moment, a diner, a trail,—simply to make our points connect.
For a decade, from a cabin at World's End,
for three from Bear Valley,
for three from Sleeping Bear Dunes—

Now, here, at White Pine, walking a winter night
towards a cabin at Wawona,
I imagine on the store's deck a phone booth, and think to call her

though the booths have all disappeared now

and think of a handset,—an incantation, a device
called forth to connect us

—what I want is the suspension of distance
where the answer can still be *yes*

when one of us says to the other *are you there*
Light

Another eve. All Saints, Halloween.
From Glacier Point, Half Dome at sunset is fired granite rose

—granite rose and gold,
and I hold my mother close, and take more photos
I will never send her again

There is something in these spaces, the in-betweens

the eves
like the twilight space in the room where my mother hovered
making her transition
at St. Pete's
Providence Saint Peter's, Olympia Washington, 9th floor

oxygen machine bubbling a quiet stream. Outside the closed door, the low hum of the nurses station. Inside, the electric murmur of dimmed lights and body-reading machines. Curtains pulled always now, to twilight the room. A Christian list on Spotify, streaming from my phone, its tiny pinhole audio aimed towards my mother's bed. Under the blankets, my hand holding hers. My hand stroking her head. On the video monitor, Providence's nature loop. I remember redwoods in mist and a brook, the redwoods especially, and knowing my mother was going to go soon. I saw us at Samuel P. Taylor, camping, in the dusk of that room, and a banner my mother always flew—*Today is the first day of the rest of your life*—and there we were at Providence, and I thought about matter, and my mother, and tried to align myself to the calm I had made in the room, and to see her already among the giant sequoias and the rain, to place her all around me, as she was so close to leaving her body, next to me, for which she was ready and I was not—

Now it is New Year's, nearly a year on
and driving from Point Reyes to Merced
here is Orion, and here are the lights,
all the low crossings to Vallejo

and I am recalling on the Brooks Range the Alpenglow,

and Limantour, the sun skating over the estero
and I hold her

across Bel Marin   across Black Point Green Point   Tolay Creek
The Napa Slough   Suisun, and a road I do not know

I wait for Crockett, the Straits, the pink neon brights of C&H
but, as often these days, I am slightly confused
in a place I thought I knew

Here is Benecia, here is Martinez,
though it's Port Costa suggested by memory

and at Carquinez, Glacier Point returns,
its hues,

—and all these eves,
there is something about suspension,
feeling her now between the lights

refinery after refinery,
nothing normally to call beautiful
off these long suspended causeways—

and it is not denial, quite, and it is not refusal... but a desire
        that everything slow,
Orion to stay suspended over the pincushions,

not to enter this final month of the first year,
not to leave behind this first year without her

—to cross and cross instead the waters on this Delta Highway, sunset
and the sun behind me now long past Inverness,
ceding westward over the Pacific, slipping the globe's curve

before me the moon rising over the slough

—for a while yet, I would like to hold here,
moving through the dark in the quiet of the evening
suspended between horizons on the dark-spanning causeways.

Susan Lively

Coming Home

Outside is in.
I shed my skin
and melt into atmosphere.
Naked and unafraid,
merging with sienna earth -
a new and better thing.
Warmth of a radiant sun
guides my way.

The animal in me
lives for life's promise;
sharp, tangy scent
of verdant grass, clean air,
and vast blue expanse
that takes away your breath
and replaces it with joy so strong,
you can taste the color yellow.

Outside is in.
I shed my skin
and move into
glittering, opaque cold.
A winter wolf on the prowl
in the moonlit satin glow
of shadowy tree sentinels
and pure winter snow.

Outside is in.
I shed my skin,
grow fins
and plunge into
salty, aqua flow
I feel myself letting go
blossoming with waves and wind,
sun and sand.
In this liquid womb
I am free again.

Outside is in.
I shed my skin,
unfold my wings;
defying death and gravity
soaring into eternity
on a cloud citadel of dreams
where peace and love reign supreme
for all of our humanity - *outside is in.*

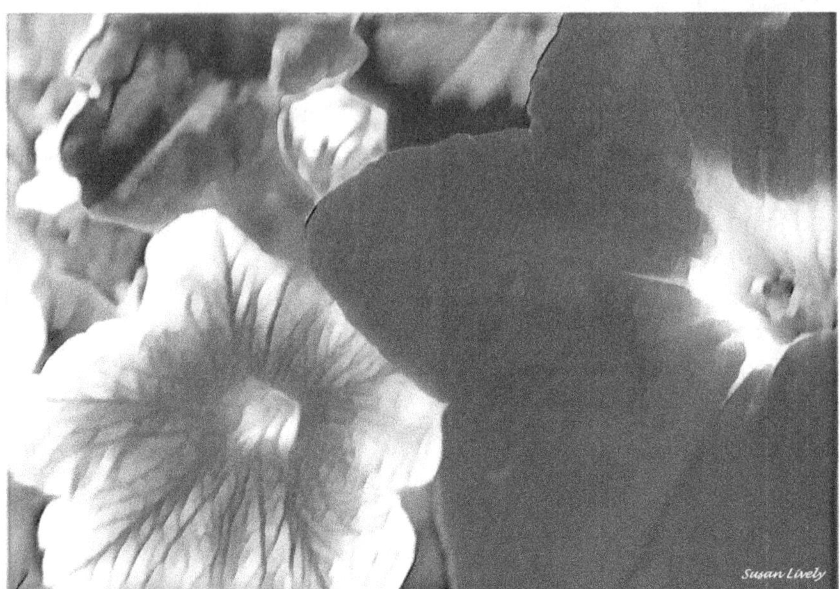

Susan Lively
Morning Glory, 2017
Photography

Jordan Mackey
A Poet's Quest

It's true what they say
About us — we have flipped through various pages,
Our eyes absorbing the words.
Our fingers smoothing the creases made by the
Careful hands before us.
Our story gently forming with a pen stroke,
The ink sinking into the paper, relieving it of its thirst.
Our mind searching for its purpose,
As we scratch out the last line, and begin again.
Its true what they say
About us—

Virginia Mallon
Wilderness of Salt

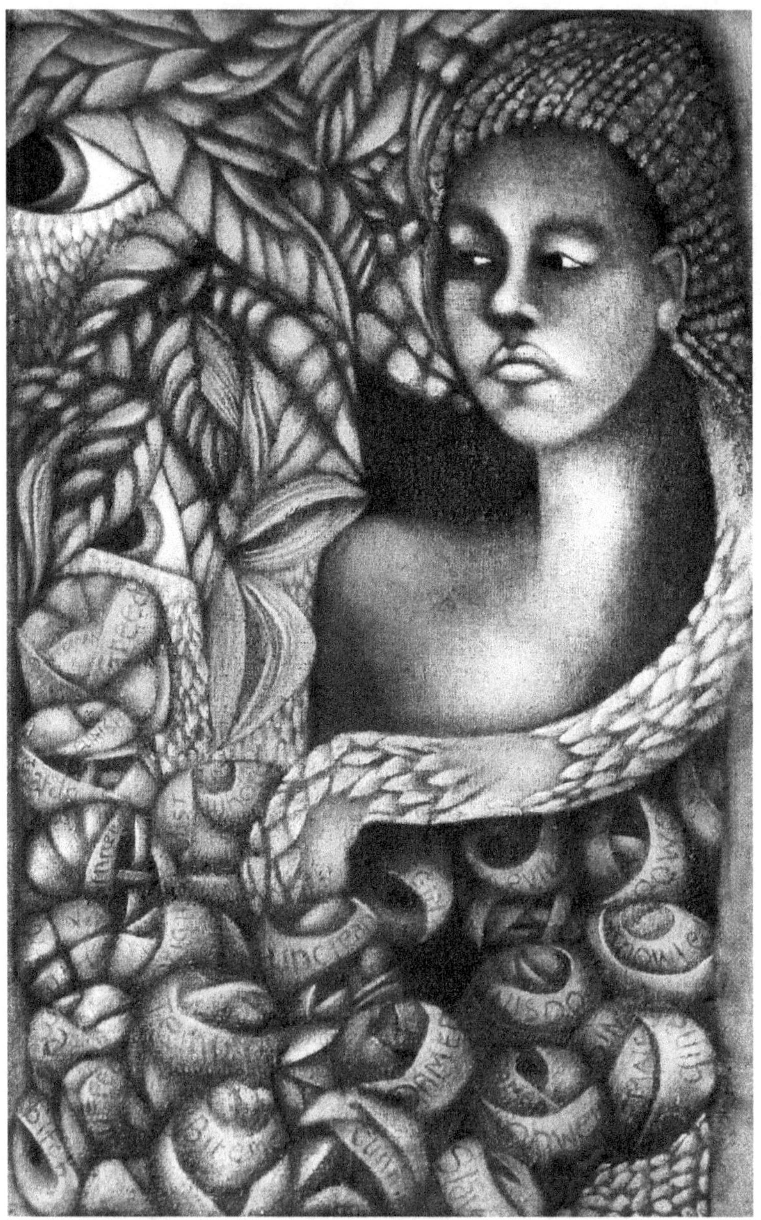

Eve in the Garden of Good and Evil,
oil on burlap with found and reclaimed objects

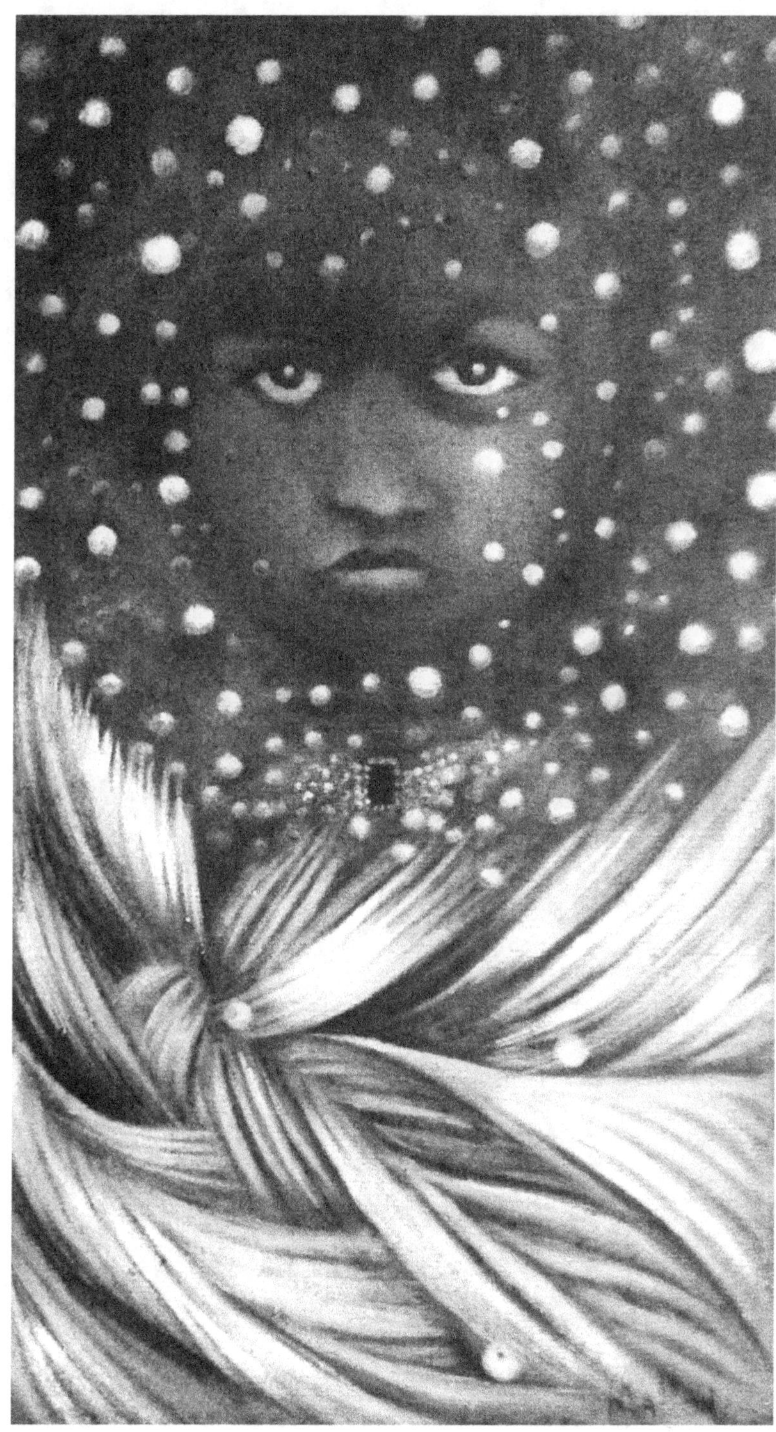

Ledal,
oil on burlap with found and reclaimed objects

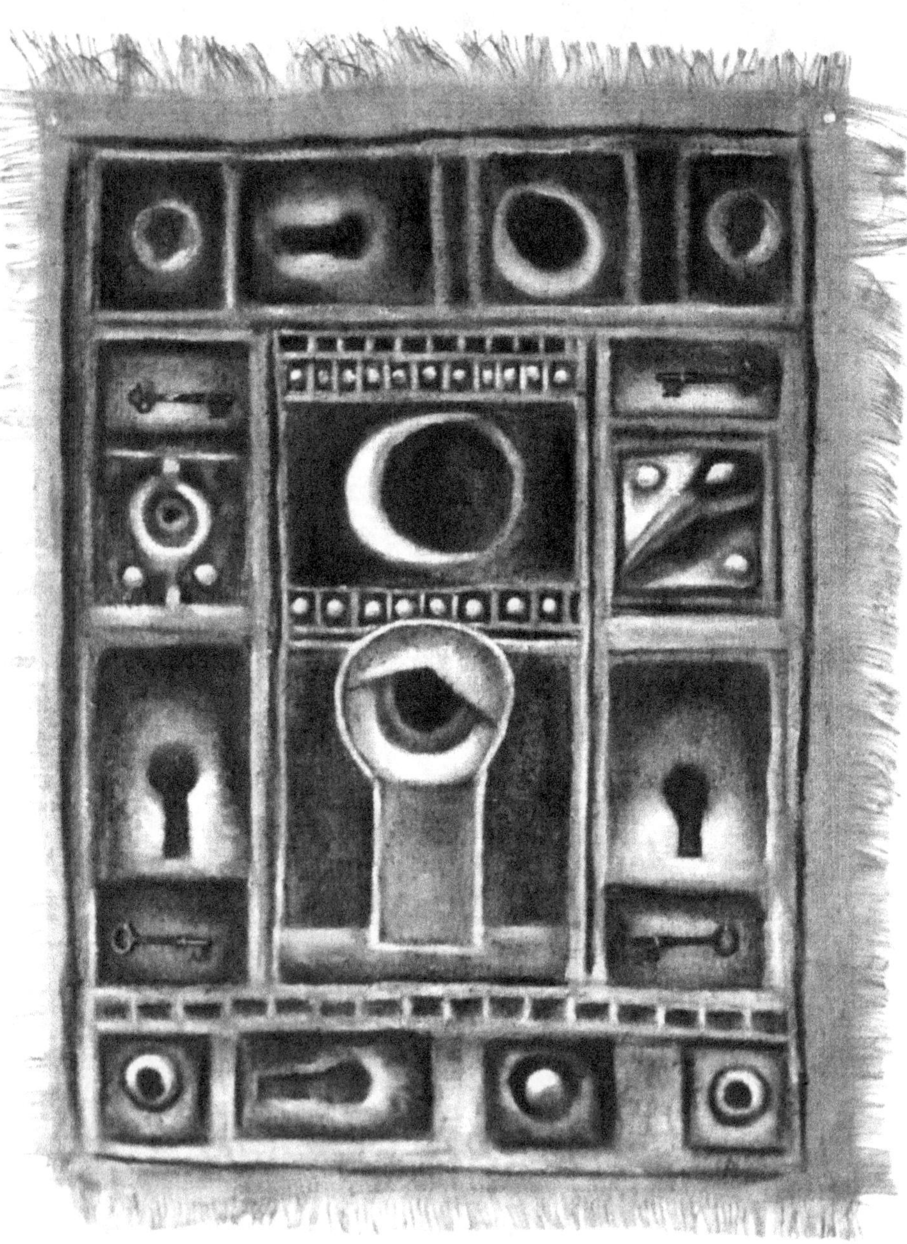

Mary Mallon Incarceration,
oil on burlap with found and reclaimed objects

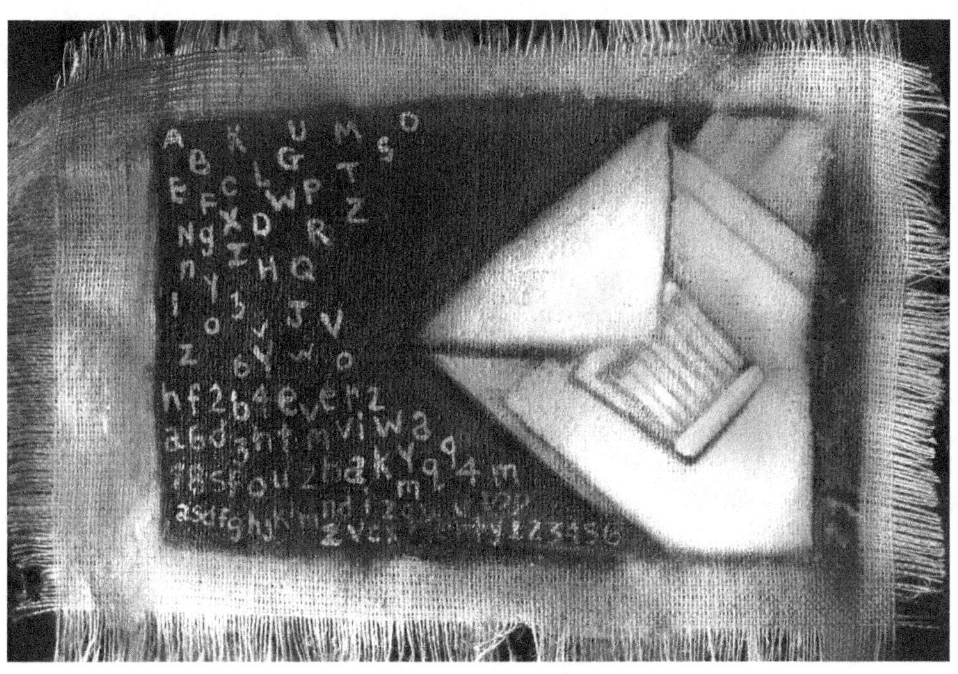

Terry Burton the Letter,
oil on burlap with found and reclaimed objects

Helena Mariño

SIX

still the terror of the flesh still
and wired around her fingers
barbed wire or the incapacity
of the body to move through
the world

to name is to unhide these places
then she won't   use a language
that can't translate el espanto

of the flesh

meh she says it doesn't matter
at the end both monstrosity
and beauty require tongue's adaptation

Olena Marukhnyak

I Remember

I remember the taste of plastic in my mouth
white, cylinder-shaped pills
sticking to the inside of my throat
I remember the fog that
enveloped me each morning
I remember the static
the quiet whisper on my mind
something unintelligible
something surreal
I remember the emptiness
the long stares
the thoughtless words
I remember the fear
dull but ever pressing
I remember existing
but I don't remember me
I remember the touch
but not its warmth
the words
spoken in whispers
the glances
shapeless and fleeting
the sound of their voices
black and white
electric
the cold wall
my back pressed against each night
that I couldn't sleep
the sharp glass bits
on the pavement
my bare feet grazed
the density
of every raindrop
on my face
as I stared upward
but through

I remember the bitter black coffee
you brought me to bed
the beads of sweat on your temples
the oversized and awkward
bureau in our bedroom
the faded blue camping chairs
on the balcony
I occupied daily
motionless
I remember counting the windows
of the abandoned hospital across the street
forty seven
but I always lost count after that
I remember the smell of your car
stale tobacco
and grief
the images of streets
you drove me through
flashing past like comic strips
I remember the coming and goings
I don't remember who
I remember almost enough
to shape reality into
a shitty collage
to scrape bits of memory
and hope they hold
with watered down glue
with plastic actions
and clouds of smoke
with colorful pills
and gray endings
I hoped to shape reality
into a known
out of something too fragile
to be concrete
I don't remember
how I got out
but I do remember
that I never forgot
to breathe

Victoria Mbabazi

Breaking Dishes

I HAD A NICE KITCHEN. The cupboards, the drawers and chairs were made of oak. Green walls, a deep green, his favourite colour. Marble tables, a grey gradient, my preferred hue. Although, the floors were checkered and shiny, the debris on the floor was green as well. I stared down at the shattered plate. He always insisted on green cutlery, said it matched the walls. Now I'm living in a home that other than the tables, only matched him.

I put my foot on the mess and pressed down. When I felt satisfied, I reached for a different plate then my phone started to ring.

It was Evelyn.

"Hey," I said clearing my throat. "I'm a little busy right now-"

"No you're not," she cut me off. "I'm at the door. I can hear you throwing shit. We all can."

"We?"

I heard a loud banging at the door.

"Isabelle," it sounded like Linda. "Let us in before you kill yourself, I wanna go to the movies."

As I opened the door Linda was about to knock again. Evelyn still had the phone to her ear, she was slightly behind her. Alice stood further to the side, leaning on my wall.

"I'm coming in," Linda said. "Evelyn, if she's no fun today I'm going to be mad. We could've just gone."

"Hey," Evelyn said to me. "You okay?"

"Of course not," I opened the door wider. "Come in."

"I was just worried."

"You're supposed to call before you come not when you're here," I said. "Get in."

Ben was perfect to a fault. His smile did more than quite reach his eyes; it had them in a choke hold. He was always so happy to see me. Even when he shouldn't be. He walked into our marriage's funeral like someone who didn't understand that the subject was dead.

We sat in the waiting room until our lawyer came for us. We were getting the separation finalized that day and he was holding his hand comforting me. Like any husband should.

"I still love you," he said. "That's never going to change."

"That's part of the problem," I said. "You don't know what this means."

"I don't care that you cheated."

"I wish that you did."

I was about to close the door after Evelyn and Linda ran inside, when I noticed Alice standing still, eyeing the floor.

"What? Aren't you coming in?"

"Your foot," she said. "It's bleeding."

"Just get inside," I said.

Alice walked in and I closed the door.

Evelyn was sitting on one of the chairs by the island. Linda was holding a broom and dust pan.

"Iz, what are you doing?" Linda asked me. "Why are you breaking things?"

"She's mad," Evelyn said. "People break shit when they're mad."

"People also murder when they're mad, does that sound sensible to you?" Linda asked trying to sweep up the mess. I took the broom away from her.

"Have you seen *He's Just Not That into You*?" I asked.

They all shook their heads.

"When Janine gets mad that her cheating husband is lying to her," I explained. "She breaks the mirror and then she picks up after herself. Why does she do that? That's totally something I would do but why? It's broken and unfixable."

"Aren't you the cheater?" Linda asked. "Shouldn't Ben be breaking dishes?"

"No," I shook my head. "I mean yes I cheated but he's the liar. He said he would stay and he didn't."

"I don't think that works," Evelyn said. "Cleaning broken shit and fixing it are two different things-"

"I'm not cleaning up a mess he made."

"Isabelle," Alice said. "You're bleeding. It's all over the floor."

"It's literally not a mess he made," Linda said trying to grab at the broom. I moved back every time, barely noticing the sting on the bottom of my foot. "You cheated. On. Him. It's your mess clean it up."

Evelyn picked me up and put me on the kitchen island. I hated being lifted but I was too mad at Linda to be mad at Evelyn.

"Oh my god," Evelyn laughed until she snorted and then laughed until she hiccuped. "Ben?"

I was driving her to the airport. We had just finished fourth year of college and she was going home to visit her mother before she settled in with her boyfriend Adam. Neither of them had a licence then, so I offered to drive her.

"Yeah," I said embarrassed. "We went on a date."

"I fucking love that," she said her grin so wide it was hurting my cheeks. "You guys are like polar opposites. Like he's so sweet and funny, it's almost annoying. You're like… "

"I'm like what?"

"Kind of a bitch."

"You don't get to judge me," I said. Linda rolled her eyes, making me angrier. "Just because you're mad your husband left you for a man."

“Actually, I do get to be mad at you,” Linda said. Alice and Evelyn bent down staring at my foot. Alice raised her eyebrow, Evelyn was biting her cheek.

“You know what that did to me,” Linda continued. “And then you do it to your perfect husband. What’s wrong with you?”

“He’s not perfect,” I said scratching my head. I looked down at the other two women, annoyed. “It’s not a big deal I stepped on a plate.”

“I think she’s gonna need stitches,” Alice said ignoring me.

“I’m not sure,” Evelyn looked away from my foot to look over at Alice. “All I see is blood.”

“Linda’s the doctor,” Alice looked up at Linda. “Does she need stitches?”

“Screw her foot,” Linda glanced down at it. “It’s not as bad as it looks. Get her rubbing alcohol and a bandaid.”

“I don’t know why you care so much,” I said to Linda. Alice got up and went looking for bandaids. “I didn’t cheat on you.”

“You’re playing victim and breaking dishes,” Linda said. “This is stupid.”

“It’s none of your business.”

“We can fix this Iz,” Ben said to me. I was cleaning that green plate three hours before it shattered. There was a little speck of food on it and no matter how hard I scrubbed the thing, it wouldn’t budge. I thought that the plate would break before it came off. I was wrong, but I broke the plate anyway.

“Then why are you leaving?” I asked. I meant to whine but it came out too casual. I was flawed to perfection. Everything in me was always screaming to keep quiet. I wasn’t a woman who begged a man to stay with me. It sent alarms off in my head. The abandonment issues were there but they were private. Revealing them was like hitting the self destruct button. I say everything calm and rational, a well oiled machine with a destruct button. A please don’t leave me button.

“We’re separated,” Ben said. “You said you didn’t want me anymore.”

“I didn’t say I didn’t want you, I said it was over,” I told him like the semantics were relevant.

“I’m not playing games,” he set a key beside the sink. “Come get me when you’re done having whatever this is.”

“Linda go help Alice find band aids,” Evelyn said standing up straight.

“I’m sure she knows where they are.”

Evelyn turned around and gave Linda a pointed look. She rolled her eyes and went after Alice.

Evelyn and I were left alone. She was staring at me so I stared back.

Close friends don’t actually have conversations with their eyes. We play charades with more subtle movements.

“Was this fuckery all you had planned for today?” Evelyn asked.

“Pretty much.”

She had her arms crossed over her chest and she kept putting her weight on each leg back and forth. It’d be less annoying if she just paced.

“I love you,” Ben’s voice was soft. Comfy like a pillow. I could rest on it, found myself always supported by the calm in his voice. I kept waiting to destroy him, never thought I’d find a man stronger than my stubbornness.

We were stretched out on the head of a boat on an island in the Caribbean. He always wanted to go on vacations. He liked the tropics just like him, colourful and warm. I liked it temperate, the sky looking like a 50s motion picture and everything cool. We were not the same but even temperate regions saw sunny days.

He was all of mine.

“So he left?” Evelyn asked me her eyes searching mine, staring right at that button.

"He said he wouldn't leave-" I started.

"And then he left," she finished.

She came closer to me and put her arms on either side of me on the table. She started tapping her fingers.

"The movie's at six," she said.

"Okay."

She backed away and then turned around facing the cupboards. When she looked back at me with that grin so wide I felt it in my face.

"Where's the expensive shit?"

I looked at the sink and saw the key right next to it, picked it up and pointed to the cupboard on the left. ☙

Jessica (Lyner) Mehta

Namesakes

My mother named me after her
father she hated. Like buying Papo's notice
with a fat grandchild would make up
for anything. My mother
named me after famous cowboys
then went and married an NDN
herself. Meanwhile her own
mother said *No*

darker. My mom named me
the second most popular girls
name in 1981 because firsts
were for good girls without
panic. My middle
name was the same as a boy
in sixth grade with greasy
nails and dirty hair so I
said it was short for Colette.
My mother was a surprise

fifteen years too late. In the hospital,
her father said, *She ain't much*
to look at, is she? and asked
the nurse to name her. The little Mexican
girl chose Rita after her own
child and nobody not nowhere ever
could say a pearl was an ugly thing.
My mother named me

for a man she despised well
after his girth had gone
to skeleton and the coffin flies
went still — but still,

I thought a namesake
should mean something
good and holy like clean
slates, buried shames and starting overs.

Guia Nocon
Casting: A Poem in Three Movements

Part 1: Map

To navigate, moths fly by the moon. They often become lost. Wayward wings chasing artificial lights blindly into windows. Dull, dumb in the effort, they don't realize the persistence of glass.

I heard a beautiful story that women once cycled with the moon. When I'm on my moon and it's just a silver sickle in the sky, I say, I'm lost, too. Lost without the benefit of wings or candle-fire.

When monarchs fly from north to south, they do not return. A whole new generation of butterflies journey back. No matter how much scientists disguise the tree, the butterflies keep coming back to the same one.

Once, I got into my car and it wouldn't start. The one that would was a row and two cars over. Yesterday, I forgot where I was born. Today, I forgot what I was here for.

Tomorrow, I'm going to follow the moon to the ocean and wonder why she won't take me back.

Part 2: Speak Violent

A child mimics speaking. Any movement of the mouth resembling speech. During choir practice, the child mouths watermelon watermelon watermelon not knowing what it means. Only that it's okay. That it's passing. Bare the teeth. Groan. The lower lip lifting upward. Sliding back. The child takes a breath. Utter something. Anything. Just one. But the breath falls, back of the throat, choking. The child gathers its shoulders. There is a ball between the shoulder blades. Pushing inwards. Making it hard to swallow. Struggling. Stubborn with last efforts against pain. The pain that wishes it to speak.

A child mimics a vessel. Waiting. Allowing others to fill. To take up residence in the mouth. To swarm and make full. They yell inside and the child struggles to hear an echo. Hoping the echoes will remain. Trapped in the barren cave now swollen. There to be used. A relay. A gasp from the pressure. The pressure of the void. The pain of it swelling. The pain of not saying. The lack of utterance.

Part 3: Crisis

May I write words more naked than flesh,
Stronger than bone, more resilient than
Sinew, sensitive than nerve.
-Sappho

Removed from me now,
this undoubtedly, will come
claiming me with violence, later.

Yet, unrealized,
immensity of the event, in the writing:
— the carving of a body
— the gouging into a body
— coldness, gasp, clenching hands
— what was thought to be calming music
— what was supposed to be a brave smile

The attempt of
what I haven't touched upon, what I can't
get close to, frustration.
Lack of necessary language
to make it still. Stop it dead in its tracks.
Declension unknown, unseen.

A rock, white as a knuckle,
sits in the stomach
waiting to be terribly upset. Waiting
to unravel the spool of my life,
tangling the threads
so they'll never comb out.

For now, keep this rock
nestled in the stomach: a
good luck token, a worry doll
tucked under a pillow.
Whisper, tip toe, lull it like a child—as
if it meant nothing, a feather-weight matter:
        of words to realize how
        brief (a kiss on the cheek of someone you maybe love)
        fleeting (a hand at the parting)
as if it won't rankle in the memory until death.

* previously published by *Rigorous* at rigorous-mag.com

Karen June Olson

THINK AGAIN

One would think
that a life of love   and good fortune
sprinkled with mistakes   of minor sorts
could lead to the so called
golden years.

Go ahead   believe
if you must   such trust
is necessary
to proceed past
winking yellow lights.

Across a room, his hair
will appear gray
in sunlight. Yours
might hold color to roots
for awhile.   Your old dog
naps more, fetches little,
whimpers in sleep.

You'll want to hold
        all the gold
you have gathered   give
witness to what departs
        in wake
of what remains.
Get out   linger
by any fence line—
        earth
recalls beauty.
Everything is temporary
        like that shiver   up your spine.

Kasey Perkins

The Swimmer

I.
In the observing afterlife
one of the sister's memories floats
to the surface, its celluloid hair billowing
through the ether
like a drowned swimmer's

and the spirits bump against
the image
like capsized boats against a corpse

II.
it's the boy
his skin brown and wet

he does a can opener into the public
pool where the children were dropped
off for a day of free childminding

hungry
they excavate quarters
at depths of thirteen feet to feed
the vending machines
wet with mold and condensation

but the boy
he climbs the diving platform
his hair is dark and plastered
across his face
his eyes big and clear
(so clear, how did they used to be
so clear)
and red from excess chlorine
and urine in the water

III.
the sister sees his toes
they're long like hers
his body still carries the chubbiness
of a few years prior
and he has all his teeth
she marvels at them now

they're white, they look at the sister
through his dark face
through the wispy edges of recollection

IV.
and the boy grins
and the water drips off his skin
and the light hits him
and hits the surface of the water
and when the boy hits

there are showers and showers of light
his point of entry

V.
elsewhere
the sister dives to see
an explosion of gold-filled bubbles
wrapped around the tan body
the boy
back dropped in the color
of municipal algae

and the spirits dive to see
the boy's grinning skull
beneath the chlorine waves

and the sister realizes
this boy is dead too

VI.
this boy
not the adult she sometimes
hated
but also this boy
who is laughing because the lifeguard
wants him to quit diving into people

who hasn't yet been to Iraq
who hasn't yet been to prison

someone in the observing afterlife
should dive down
and warn him
about the man who will sever his thumbs

(they're so young and pruny
in the cool blue water)

and stab him
and leave him to bleed out
on the floor of the grandmother's house.

Olivia Serio

Proverbs 30:16

> *There are three things that will*
> *not be satisfied, four that will*
> *not say, "enough": the barren*
> *womb; the grave; the earth that*
> *is not filled with water; and fire.*

he says I am like the desert
barren and cursed—no

descendants to find the sticky sweet
milk that flows freely. a promise made

to someone who will never know its truth.
I strike the stone twice and the water both

sustains and condemns. I will never
know what it is like to be chosen

and my soles will crack with
the weight of heaven.

***

he says I am like the desert—
bleached bone white, a carcass picked

clean, nothing left to sustain
even the most indifferent of suitors.

but he knows only the heat, the unrelenting
sun. no knowledge of the world

in the dark, the juice that runs thick
with understanding, with life.

he does not know of the life after
daylight, of the renewal it brings.

***

he says I am like the desert: all
grit and heat, but I am too in love

with the stars for that to be a bad thing.
the deep darkness, the dust, like I'm

back at the beginning, like my bones feel
the memory of what they used to be.

***

he says I am like the desert.
swept bare like the blaze that burns

clean, the final promise fulfilled:
what was once ash is now rich earth.

he sends a pillar of flame to light the dark
but I know my way around the shadow;

I am the way, the truth, the life, no one comes
into fatherhood except through me,

there is no life without the fertile
fruit that comes through this fire.

Kristen Sharp
Changed My View

I finally made the decision to change
sides of the bed with my lover—
Seems strange I didn't make this decision sooner
and realized that I had also changed my view
When I had slept by the window
I was staring out at an old tower building renewed
of concrete, brick and artificial light
that glowed upward
which lit the skyline at night
When I chose to move
to the right side of the bed
while climbing into my sheets
I grabbed the pillow to prop up my head
I looked out the same wooden tattered lopsided window
that stammers and creaks
I saw much more than I expected
so much more
that I couldn't believe
Long trees with brown leaves still dangling off their limbs
If I look hard enough
I can see a thousand faces with full round chins
in the branches with their fall colorful flares
Birds soaring dreamlike turns of wings in air
Set in front of a black blue sky with clouded white speckled hair
And I remembered who I was
I found who I am
when I chose to look there

Sara Swinson
Paintings

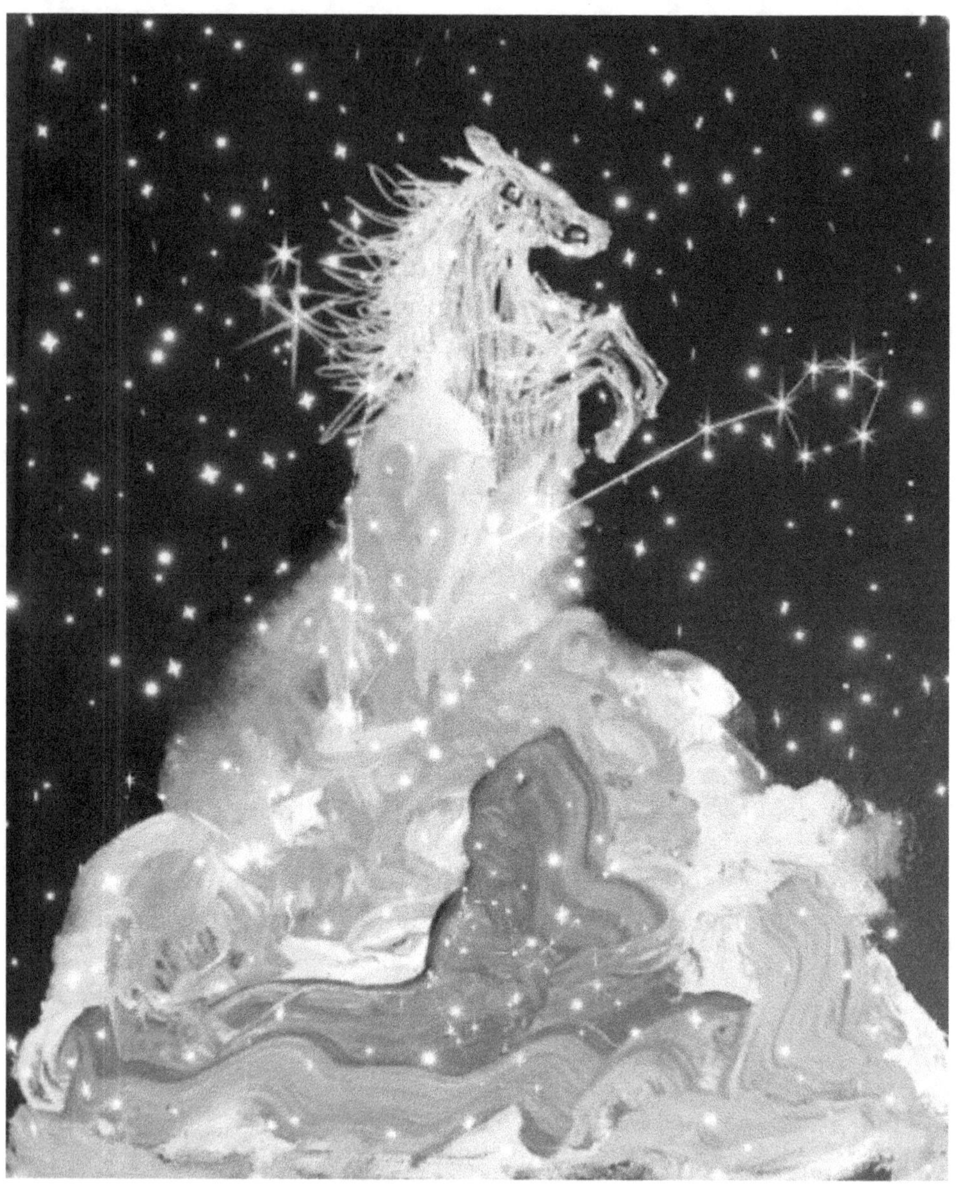

Rising Up, 2021

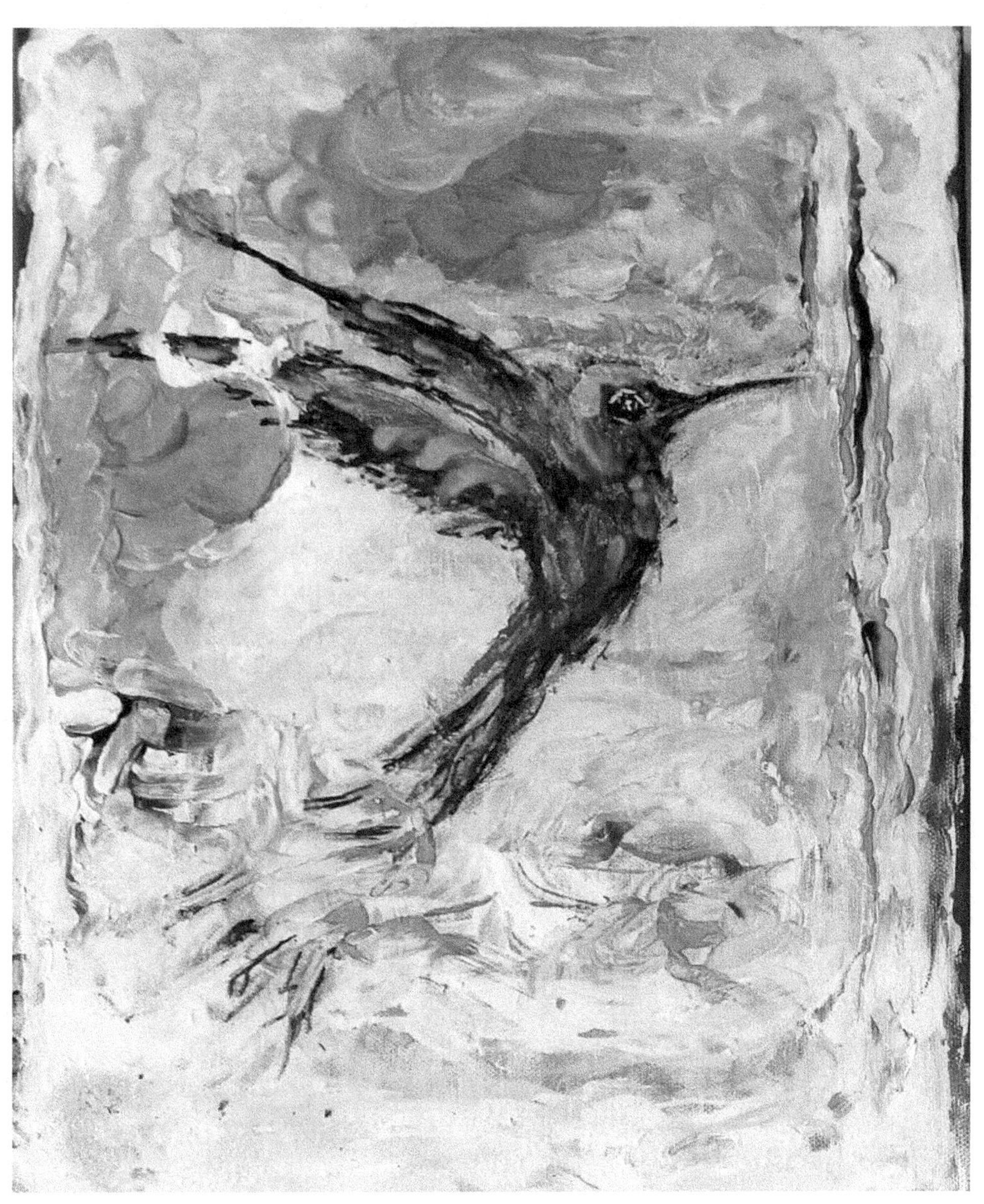

Freely, 2016

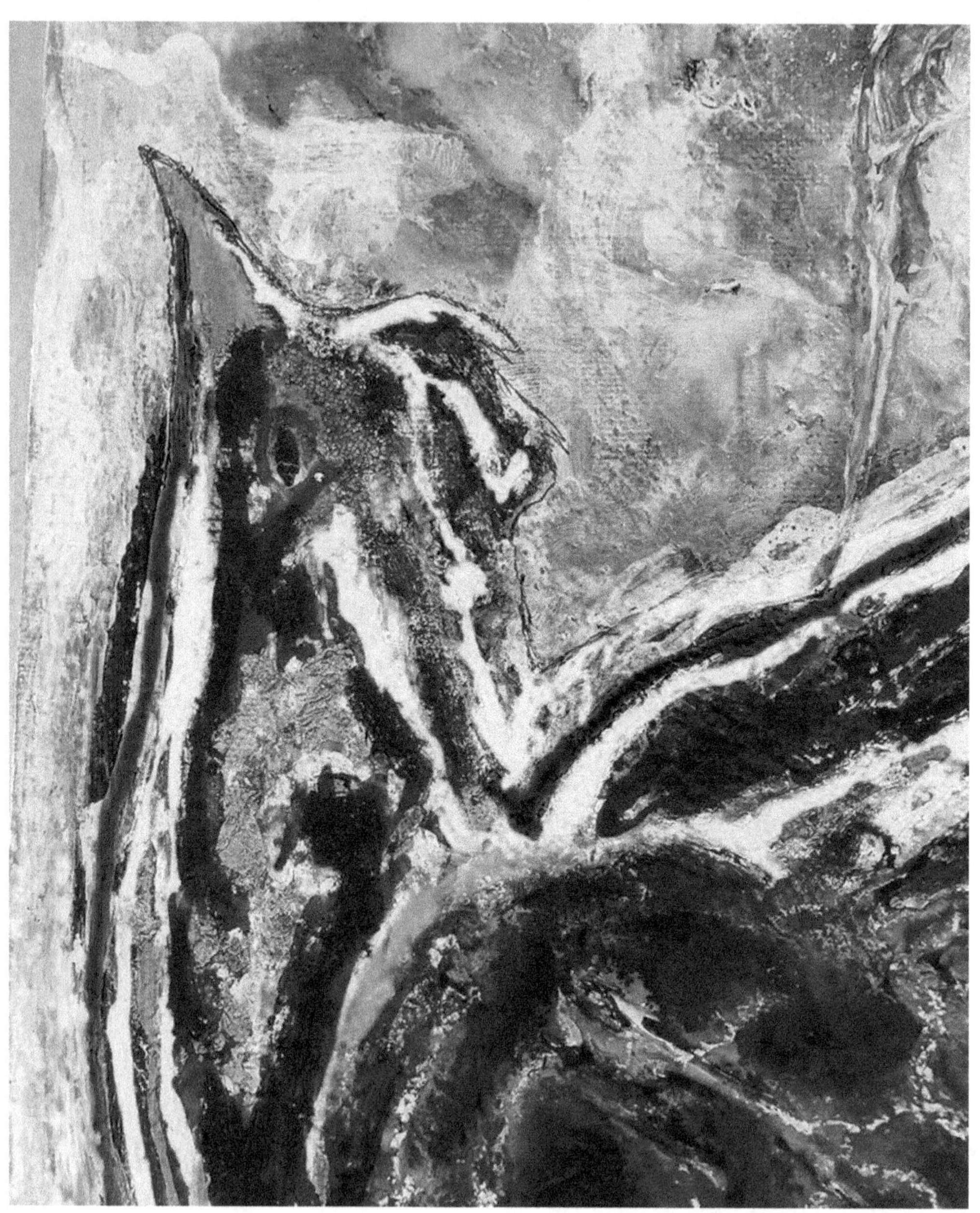

Healing in the Wounded Wings, 2020

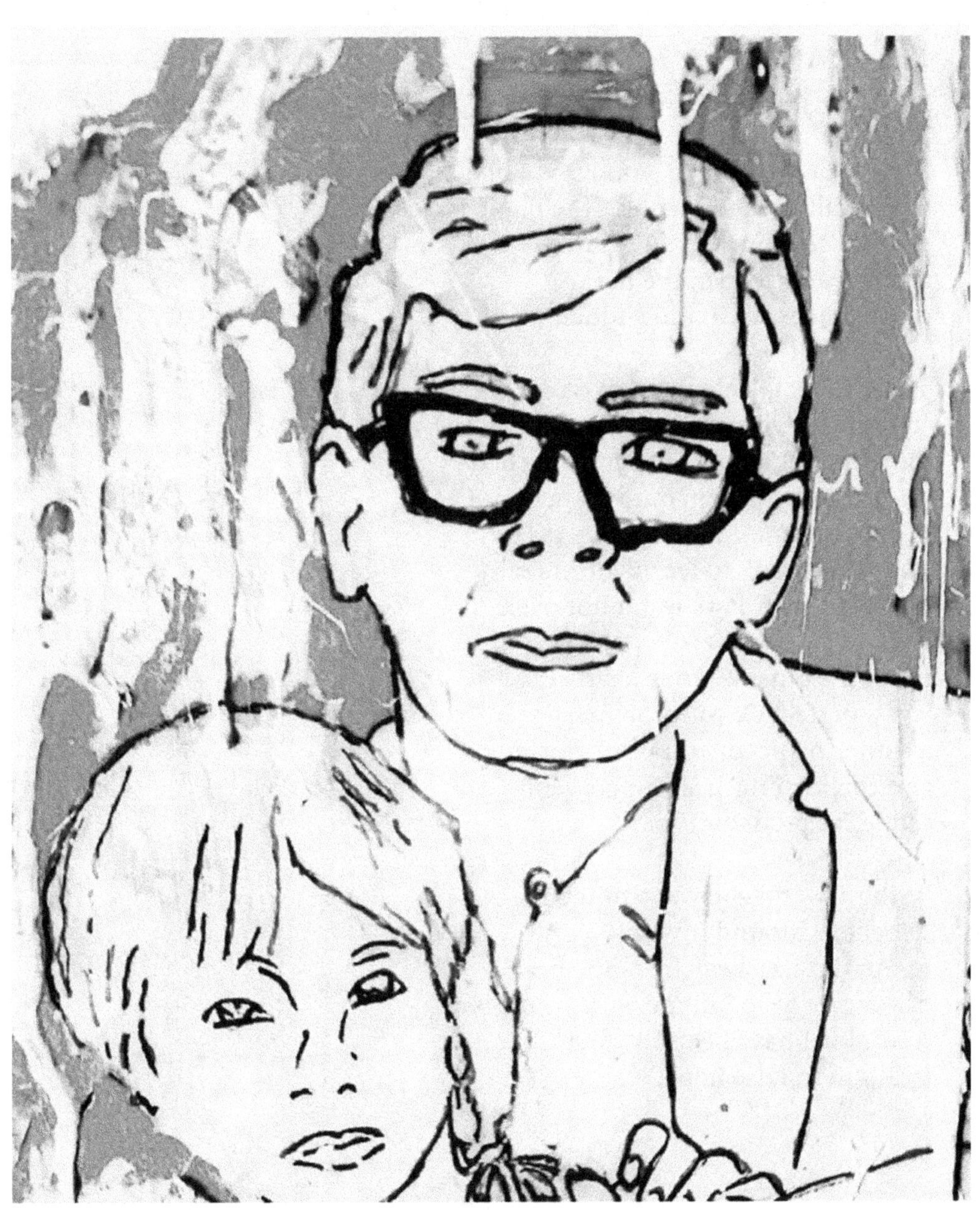

I Would Have Been A Good Daughter, 2010

Alene Terzian-Zeitounian

Postpartum

When you were born, you were a boa
who swallowed me whole. The panic
and praise, I bucked and clawed
against your throat; the dark
completeness of it, too sudden.

Then, I was the elephant in St. Exupery,
standing in your sack. They mistook me
for a mother, and I let them. I inched
toward your mouth, but you held me,
your lungs, an inflated gate.
The year it took to learn your breath,
to spread your jaws was a hot oven.

From the outside, your head,
was a perfect O, your tongue,
a slithering need. You were glorious
and threatening, a shiny, golden,
seductive predator.

In the end, maybe you wanted me
to believe I found my way
to the surface, away from the bog
of your belly, to lull me with your hiss;
it wouldn't have been the first time
I gave in to false hope.

Myrta Vida

A Daydream of You in Water, My Ancestor

I had a daydream of you
as you swayed on the first lands,
across knotty savannas
to get to the perfect river
given by the gods.
To bathe in revered waters.

You arrived to pay your tributes.
I saw your hands become
porringers to drink,
you opened lovely guava lips
as you drank.

Ancestor, I thought of your face
how it was a marvel that day,
cheeks the shade of ripe mango.
Spirit stubborn like moringa.

You danced with sun and water.
You lifted your Orisha
and friend and kin joined you,
all of them lithe and free
just like you.

I thought of you
as you stood there
veiled in the flawless river.
Radiant. Impeccable.
Surrounded by your loves
as you all praised Olorun
for the sacred and simple pleasures.

Bronwyn Voth

NATURAL SELECTION

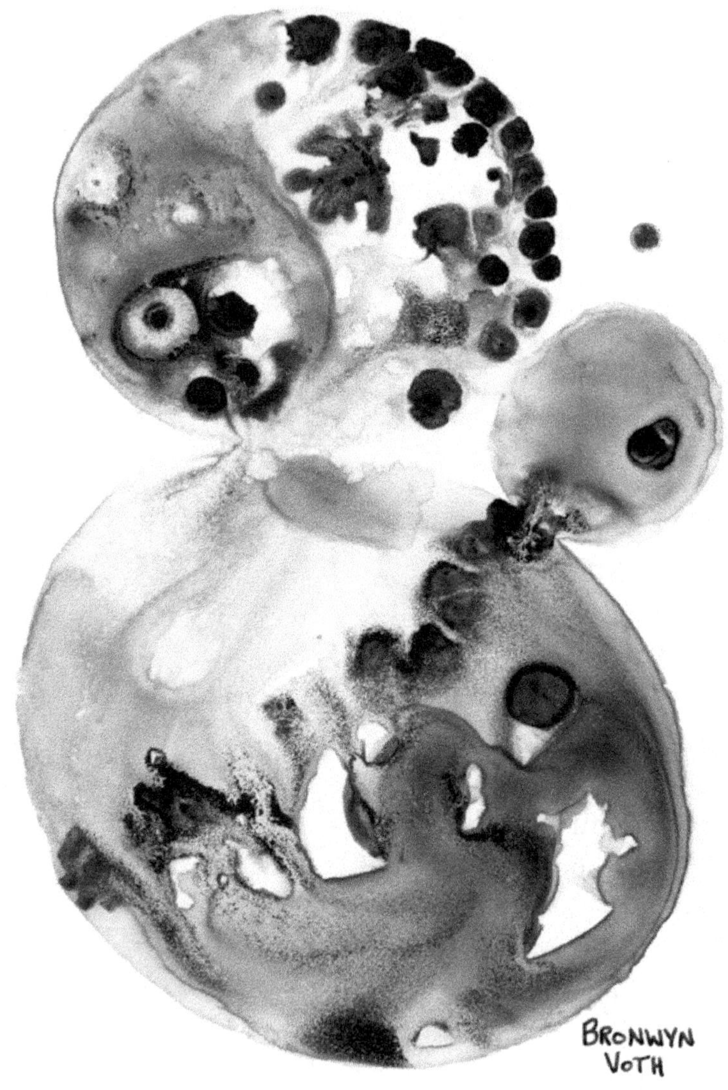

Cellularis, 2021
Alcohol ink and watercolor
on polypropylene resin

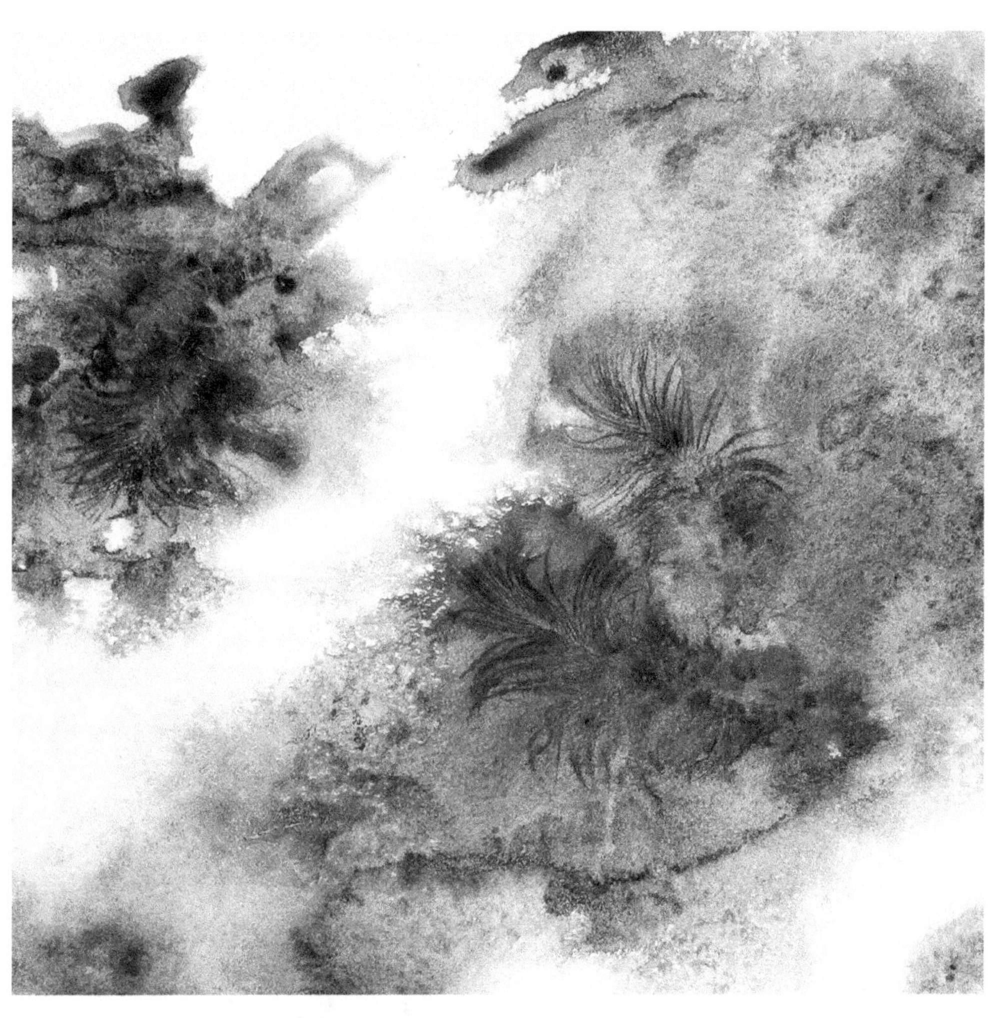

Wounded Bird, 2020
Watercolor on paper

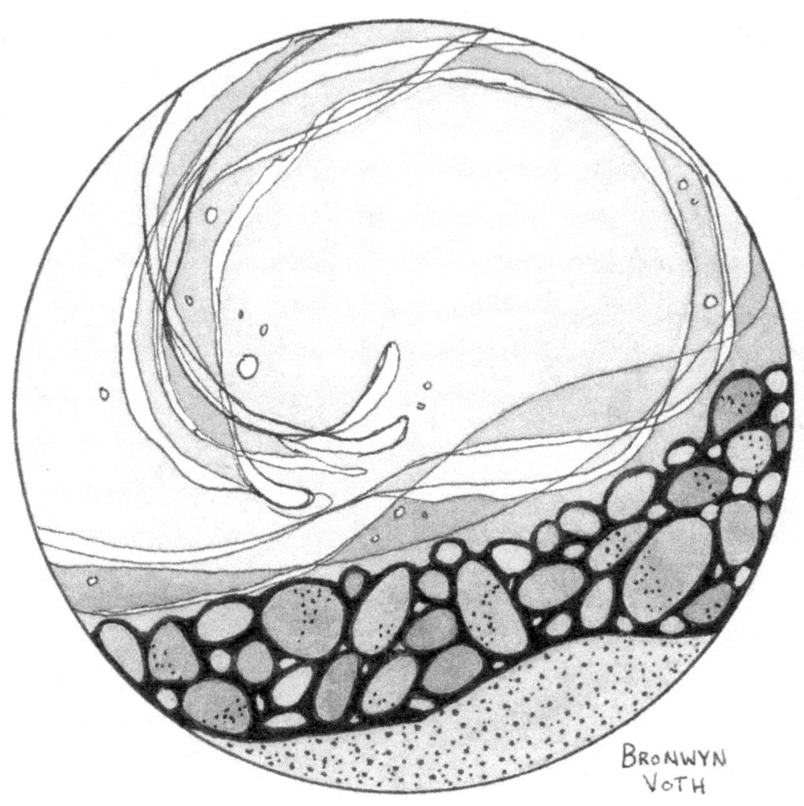

Curl, 2020
Watercolor and ink on paper

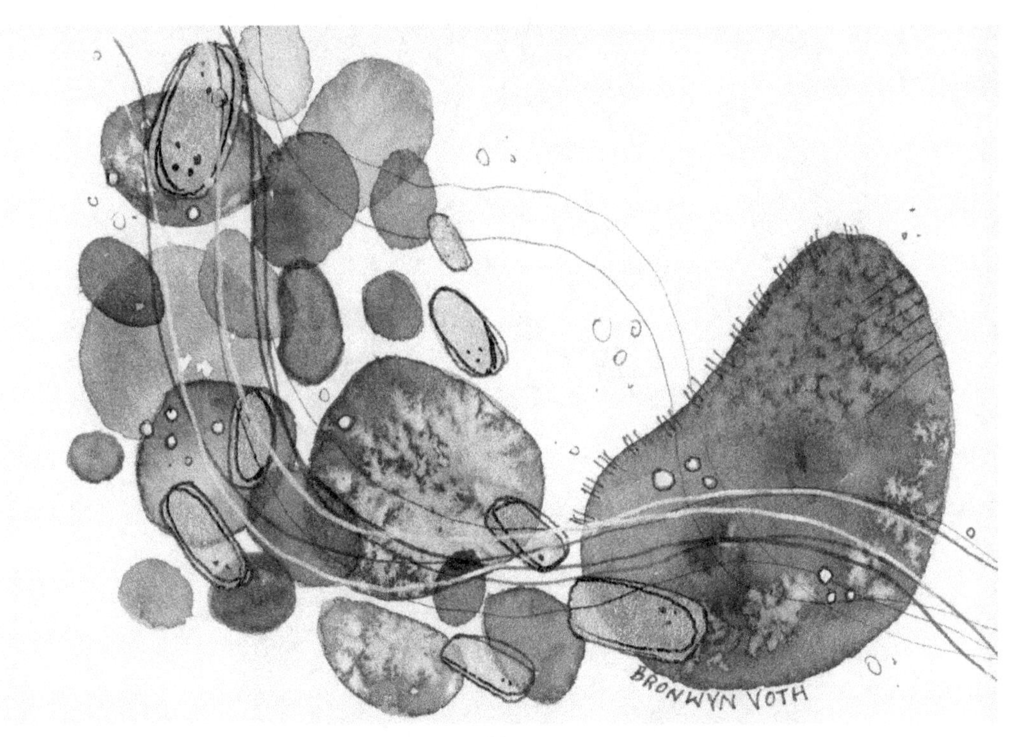

Flow: Gold in the Water, 2020
Watercolor and ink on paper

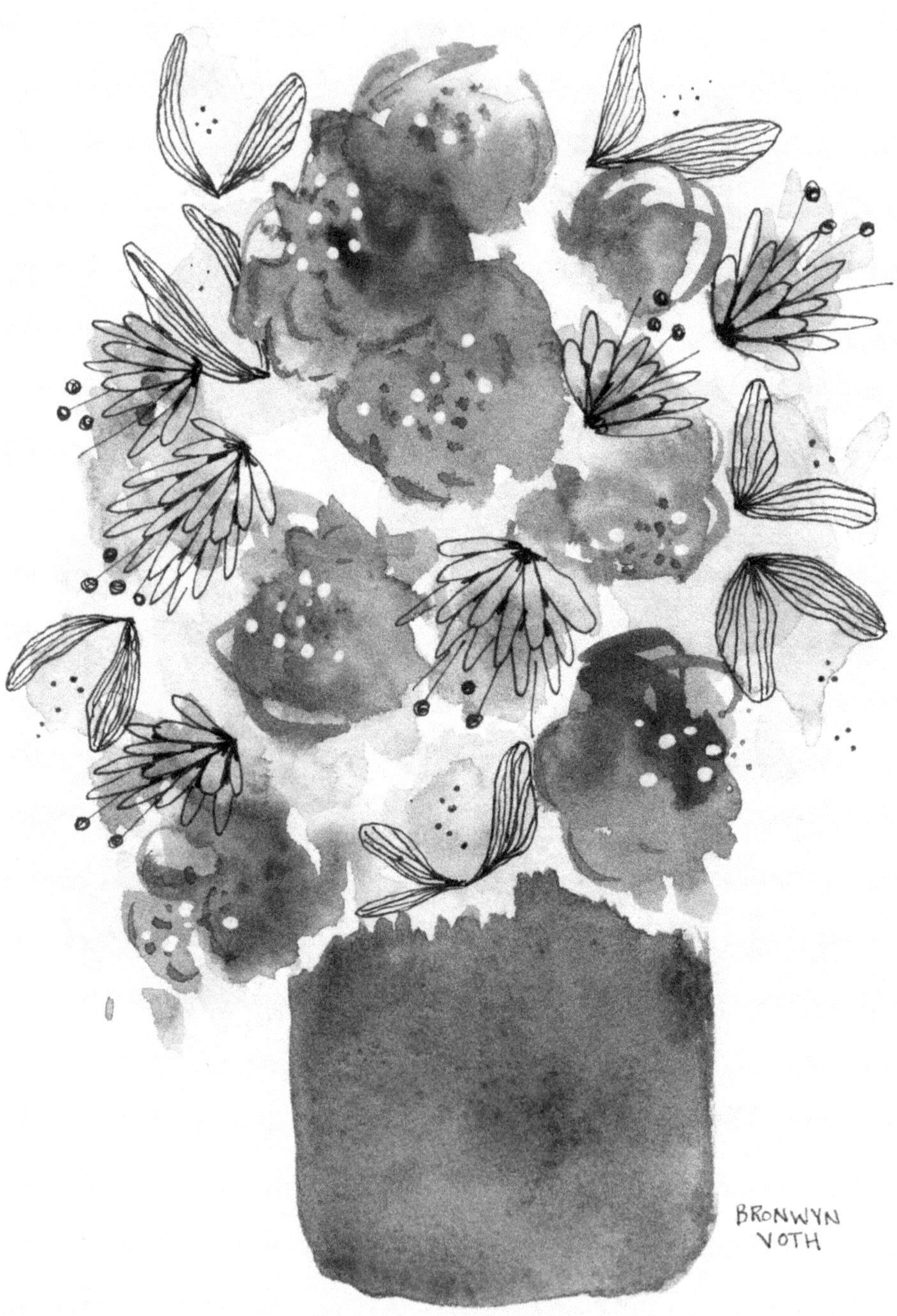

Floral - Gentle, 2020
Watercolor and ink on paper

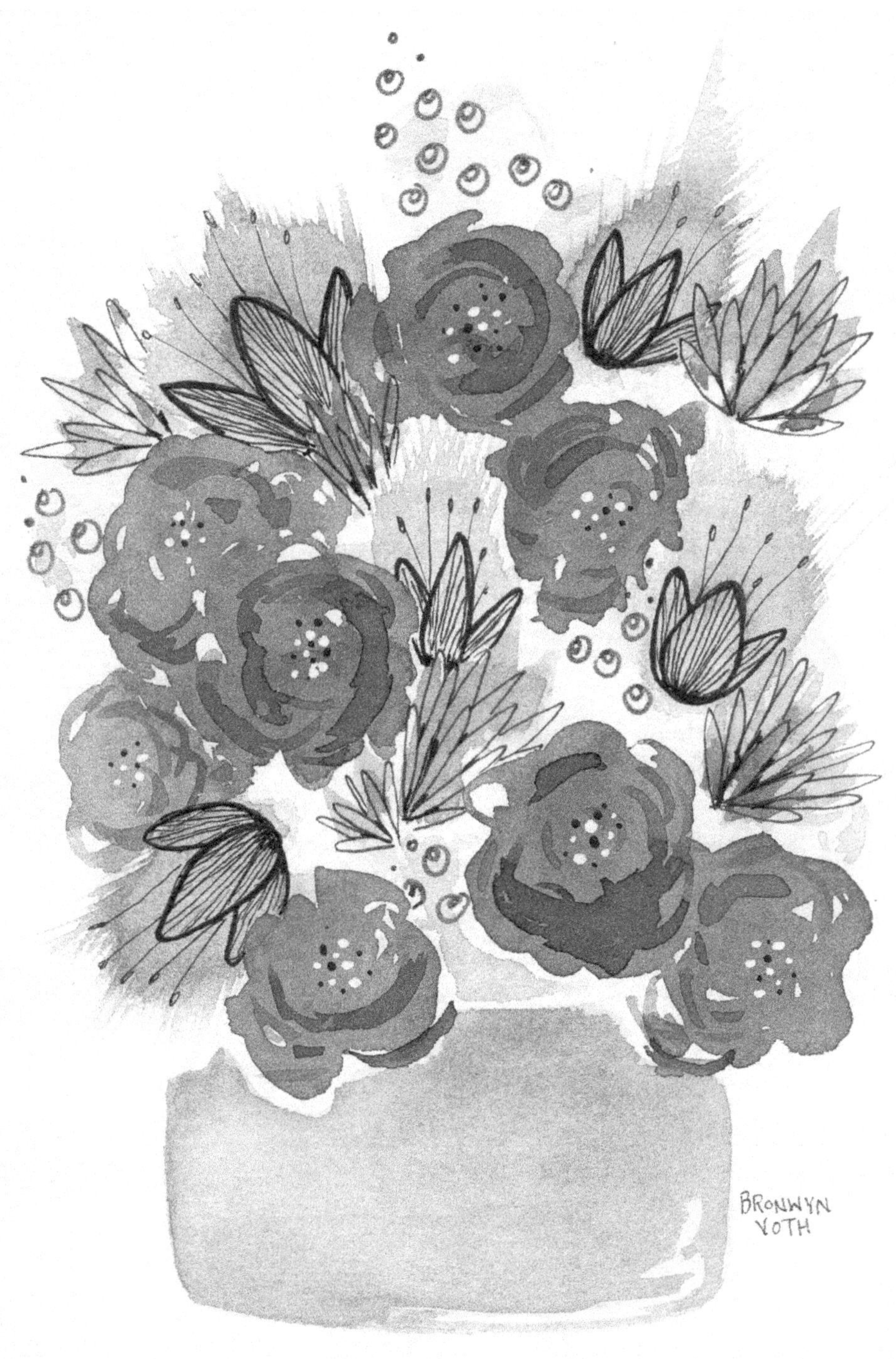

Floral - Lively, 2020
Watercolor and ink on paper

Amanda Wells

Kansas City Haiku

Three travel trunks stuffed
decades of woman grit, primed
for the unpacking.

☙

Cracking weathered spines
awakens dusty, dazzled
daydreams and doldrums.

☙

Billboard obstructions
scream, cries we leave behind
no rearview regrets.

☙

Sojurning sisters
string words heavy in our breasts,
songs of birds on wires.

☙

Suff'ring wanderlust
we confjure wildflower fields
count petals like miles.

☙

Rapt with bated breath,
prohibition reverie
awaits on exit.

Joely Williams

Chingada

Maria shook Earth's surface
Over political commonality
Harvest of fruit; vegetables
Burdened by the ruins of its constituents.
Entireties arid, faces, land, oceans, lakes, rivers, bodies.
Islands integrated illumination now follies.
Those corners we once honored ravaged by Maria's
indiscriminate misanthropy.
Arteries lacerated
Streets slashed
Directions dopey
Removing the barks of life
Visible now the restrictions
The flow of things the suppression
of their own government
I mean Guajataca Dam
Municipalities of broken pieces;
A female whose mother drowned her: La Llorona
Maria raising her cry's louder for her lost children
Inaccessible Roads that they used to invade with ease
Same roads bleed from the remains of the past
The place where the ropes buried deep
Two thousand people rescued
She hit that town the hardest.
They say she was unpredictable
She says, "I knew exactly what I was doing".
Climbing into the submerged beds.
Like they submerged Maria.

Contributor Notes

KELLI ALLEN's work has appeared in numerous journals and anthologies in the US and internationally. She is an award-wining poet, editor, and dancer. She is the recipient of the 2018 Magpie Award for Poetry. Allen's latest book is *Leaving the Skin on the Bear*, (C&R Press 2022). She currently teaches writing and literature in North Carolina.

JEANNE ALLISON loves to write poetry in stolen and in-between moments. Her work has appeared in *The Write Launch*, *Skylight47*, *Light: A Journal of Photography & Poetry*, and many others. She lives in St. Louis, Missouri, with her husband and daughter, and she teaches at the University of Missouri-St. Louis.

TANI ARNESS has enjoyed living in New Mexico for the over 20 years. She is currently the principal of Cesar Chavez Community School. A collection of her poems can be found in *Tzimtzum: 5 contemporary poets lend us their hearts* by Mercury Heartlink Press and numerous other publications. Her website is: www.tani-arness.com

MARÍA T. BALOGH is a bilingual, bicultural poet, fiction writer, Caribbean folkloric dancer, doodler/painter, and educator. She has a book of poetry in Spanish, *Bailar caribeño*, by a Spanish publisher, & a book of poetry and fiction in English, *Cumbia Soul*, (Cool Way Press). She teaches Spanish at the University of Missouri St. Louis.

REBECCA KIWI BARNSTIEN is deeply devoted to experimental poetry and voicing that which our language is ill-equipped to express. She is interested in how reader engagement changes a text. She holds a BFA from Naropa University and an MFA from the University of Kent. She has a permanent address, a cat, and a lover in Denver, Colorado.

LAUREN BECK is a project manager and editor of master's theses and novels. She is a St. Louis native. Though she has published academic and creative prose, "Knowing" is her first published poem. Lauren is currently working on a play, *Our Tina*, which delves into the themes of romance, heartbreak and renewal in Lewy body Dementia.

MICHELLE CHEN takes inspiration for her writing from the events that occur in and around her home, New York City, though she was born in Singapore and hopes to return and visit someday. Her work has appeared in *Prairie Schooner*, *Bat City Review*, *Rattle*, and elsewhere. She is currently a senior at Stony Brook University.

DAWN DUPLER's poetry has been posted on the buses of St. Louis and its MetroLink trains. Her poetry has been in journals such as *Tar River Poetry, Natural Bridge, Moon City Review, Paper Nautilus, Chiron Review, Whiskey Island*, and others. She has an MFA in Creative Writing and teaches at St. Louis Community College after retiring early from a career in engineering.

RENEE EMERSON is the author of the poetry collections *Keeping Me Still* (Winter Goose Publishing 2014), *Threshing Floor* (Jacar Press 2016), and *Church Ladies* (Fernwood Press 2023). She is also the author of the middle grade novel *Why Silas Miller Must Learn to Ride a Bike* (Wintergoose Publishing 2022). She lives in the Midwest with her husband and children.and she can be found online at www.reneeemerson.wordpress.com

JILL EVANS (aka Jill Evans Petzall) is an award-winning writer, documentary filmmaker, artist, and teacher. She holds a master's in Philosophy. After a crippling cancer recurrence at 77, she began to publish her poems. She writes and creates with the belief that only art can provide the clarity, compassion, and insights that are missing in the world.

BEVERLY FESHARAKI is a teacher/poet transformed into a poet/teacher. Her poems have appeared in *Typishly, Moria*, and many others, and the anthology, *Women Writing: On The Edge of Dark and Light*. She is a member of Inscape Poets in Tacoma, Washington and writes with Poets on the Coast in LaConner. Beverly lives in Mukilteo, Washington.

MICHELLE LIZET FLORES is a graduate of FSU and NYU creative writing programs. She is a teacher and co-hosts the What's in a Verse Poetry Open Mic in Jacksonville, FL. A finalist for the Juan Felipe Herrera Award for Poetry, she is the author of the chapbooks *Cuentos from the Swamp* and *Memoria*, and the picture book, *Carlito the Bat Learns to Trick or Treat*. Find out more at michellelizetflores.com

JESSICA FREEMAN has published work in *Mississippi Review, The McNeese Review, Third Coast, SWWIM*, and many others. She is a Pushcart Prize nominee and received an Honorable Mention from the Academy of American Poets. She is a former winner of the Joanne Hirschfield Memorial Poetry Prize.

JENNIFER GOLDRING is a writer, photographer, and editor based in St. Louis. On her days off, she can be found playing with clay, taking photos, hanging with her teenagers, or writing poems. She's Managing Editor for *december* magazine. Her award-winning poetry has appeared in various publications, and her writing, photography, and other work can be found at jennifergoldring.com.

ABIGAIL FOX GREEN is a poet and psychotherapist based in St. Louis, Missouri. When she's not working, you'll find Abigail practicing hand building ceramics, writing, or planning her next travel adventure with friends. Her work can be found in various publications.

LIBERTY HEISE is based in San Antonio, TX. Her work has been published in *Fourth River, Crate, Horse Less Review,* and many others. She was a fellow at Squaw Valley Community of Writers, Juniper Summer Writing Institute and Callaloo Creative Writing Workshop.

NASHEETAH HOSSAIN is an author and a journalist. She has a thriving love for poetry. Her hobbies are traveling and swimming.

ANASTASIA JILL (she/they) is a queer writer living in the Southeast United States. She has been nominated for Best American Short Stories, Best of the Net, and several other honors. Her work has been featured with *Poets.org, Pithead Chapel, Contemporary Verse 2, OxMag, Broken Pencil,* and more.

DEBBIE KOETJE KELLY is a Michigan woman living in Missouri. She's been writing privately for over 50 years and in small writing circles for the last few. Debbie's work is inspired by her middle school students, wild yard, bodies of water, animal encounters, social justice/injustice, and family - original, grown, and chosen. Her dogs, Pepper and Cody, serve as muses and spiritual advisors.

BELINDA KREMER is the author of *Decoherence: Poems*, and numerous chapbooks & artist's books. Her work has been featured in numerous publications. She has been poetry editor of *CONFRONTATION: The Literary Magazine,* since 2006. She has an MFA in Poetry from the University of Michigan. She won the Hopwood Major Award for Poetry. She's faculty in UC Berkeley's College Writing Programs.

SUSAN LIVELY is a producer, writer, photographer, visual artist, educator, and activist from Illinois. Co-organizer of "100,000 Poets & Musicians for Change – St. Louis", Susan also produces the series' "First Bloom" and "Women For Peace". Susan's art has been featured at Urb Arts, Mokabe's, and others. Her work has been published in numerous publications including *Extreme: An Anthology for Social & Environmental Justice.*

JORDAN MACKEY is a teacher and has a BA in English. She is a recent Cameron University Alum. She's had multiple nonfiction and poetry pieces published in a variety of journals. She hopes that her writing is a source of insight and hope for those struggling with the same demons she did as a child.

VIRGINIA MALLON is a NY artist who works with paint, photography, and occasionally mixed media. Her work contemplates religious, historic, and mythological women, the current state of the world, personal and polticial histories, and psychological undercurrents of contemporary society. Her work can be found at virginiamallon.com

HELENA MARIÑO was born in Madrid, Spain. She has an MFA in Spanish Creative Writing from the University of Iowa. Her poems have most recently appeared in *The American Journal of Poetry, GFT press, Ají Magazine*, and *El Coloquio de los Perros.*

OLENA MARUKHNYAK is a writer and educator in Brooklyn, New York. Her work centers around elevating queer and immigrant voices, as well as normalizing conversations about mental health.

VICTORIA MBABAZI is an MFA candidate with a concentration in poetry at NYU. Her work can be found in *The Puritan, CV2, Untethered Magazine*, and many others. Her poetry placed second in *The Hart House Review* contest and her work has been shortlisted in *Plenitude's* Flash Fiction contest. Her first poetry collection *chapbook* is out with Anstruther Press. To see more visit victoriambabazi.ca

JESSICA (TYNER) MEHTA, PhD is an Aniyunwiya, multi-award-winning inter-disciplinary author and artist. She is a citizen of the Cherokee Nation, but born in the occupied [read: stolen] land of what is today often called Oregon, space, place, and ancestry are the driving factors in her work. She is a Fulbright Nehru Senior Scholar in Bengaluru where she is teaching poetry workshops. Learn more at www.thischerokeerose.com.

GUIA NOCON studied poetry at the University of California, Santa Cruz. After spending most of her adult life in San Francisco and Oakland, she currently travels around the United States, working and writing on the road. Her work has appeared in *Be About It Press*, Mt. Hood Community College's journal, *Perceptions, Garbanzo Literary Journal* out of Ohio, and many others.

KAREN JUNE OLSON is Professor Emerita of Early Care and Education at St. Louis Community College. Her poems have appeared in *The 2River View, The Mas Tequila Review, Third Wednesday, Tipton Poetry Journal*, and *UCity Review*. Her chapbook, *Living Midair* can be found at 2river.org

KASEY PERKINS is a professor, freelance editor, and writer. She has her MFA in poetry from the University of Missouri – St. Louis, and she received her MA in English at Truman State University. She is the recipient of the 2014 Margaret Leong Children's Poetry Prize. Her chapbook, *When the Dead Get Mail*, was released through Finishing Line Press in 2019. You can find her at kaseyperkins.com

OLIVIA SERIO earned a BA in English and Creative Writing from Washington College in 2017 and is currently working toward a Masters in Modern and Contemporary Fiction from the University of Westminster. Her work has appeared in *THAT Literary Review, Funicular Magazine*, and *Texas Review Press*, among others. She currently resides in London with her two cats Jane and Lizzie.

KRISTIN SHARP is a poet, writer, MSW, activist, producer, and photographer originally from Saint Louis. She moved to Los Angeles, but now lives as a digital nomad and currently resides in Portugal. She produced and co-produced Poems, Prose and Pints and St. Louis, 100 Thousand Poets for Change. She has performed nationally and internationally, and her poetry and writings have appeared in various literary publications and anthologies.

SARA SWINSON is an artist and writer living in Washington, DC. A child of Foreign Service parents, she enjoyed living in other countries and taking in the culture and creative influences around her. Sara's art has been featured in film and print. She works as a Hospice Chaplain and Spiritual Counselor. Themes that intrigue her are power in vulnerability, freedom of expression, pursuing unknowable colors, healing through art, and painting as prayer. Find her on Instagram @saraswinsonart

ALENE TERZIAN-ZEITOUNIAN received an M.A. and M.F.A. in Creative Writing with an emphasis in poetry. Her first book, *Deep as City's Ache*, explores the Lebanese Civil Conflict both environmentally and psychologically. She is completing her EdD from Arizona State University, while serving as the English Department Chair at College of the Canyons. She is the faculty advisor of COC's award-winning literary and arts magazine, *cul-de-sac*. Her poems have appeared in *The Colorado Review, Cordite, Levitate, Media Cake, Cathexis, Duende,* and *Rise Up Review* to name a few.

MYRTA VIDA (Meer-Tah Vee-Dah) was born and raised in Puerto Rico, is a decorated Army Veteran, writer, and producer. She earned her MFA in Creative Writing from the University of Missouri –St. Louis. Now Brooklyn-based, she teaches Screenwriting at NYFA's NYC campus, and is a Story Consultant for Independent Filmmakers. She's led writing workshops for a variety of groups, to include: her fellow Veterans, at-risk youth, survivors of domestic violence, the elderly, and the LGBTQ+ community.

BRONWYN VOTH is a watercolor artist living in Missouri. She finds inspiration in the natural world and her work is filled with flowers, feathers, stones, and mushrooms. She is an avid gardener and self-taught naturalist. She lives in St. Louis and loves teaching others about the natural world. You can find her art at bronwynvoth.com

AMANDA WELLS is a poet, educator, and professional development consultant living in St. Louis, Missouri. She uses language and her career experience to help women pursue liberation and joy in their own unique ways. For better or worse, her work has been published in various places over the last 15 years.

JOELY WILLIAMS was born and raised in Bronx, N.Y and now lives in Columbia, SC. She loves to write about life and spiritual experience. She started her writing debut focusing on all things trains in NYC for Trainsnyc.com and expanded to producing works for BMCC and Brooklyn College newspapers and magazines. She was also featured on the *Writers Guild: Uncanny* magazine and well as *Weirdo Brigade Magazines*. She is a mom of two and is working on publishing an anthology of poetry.

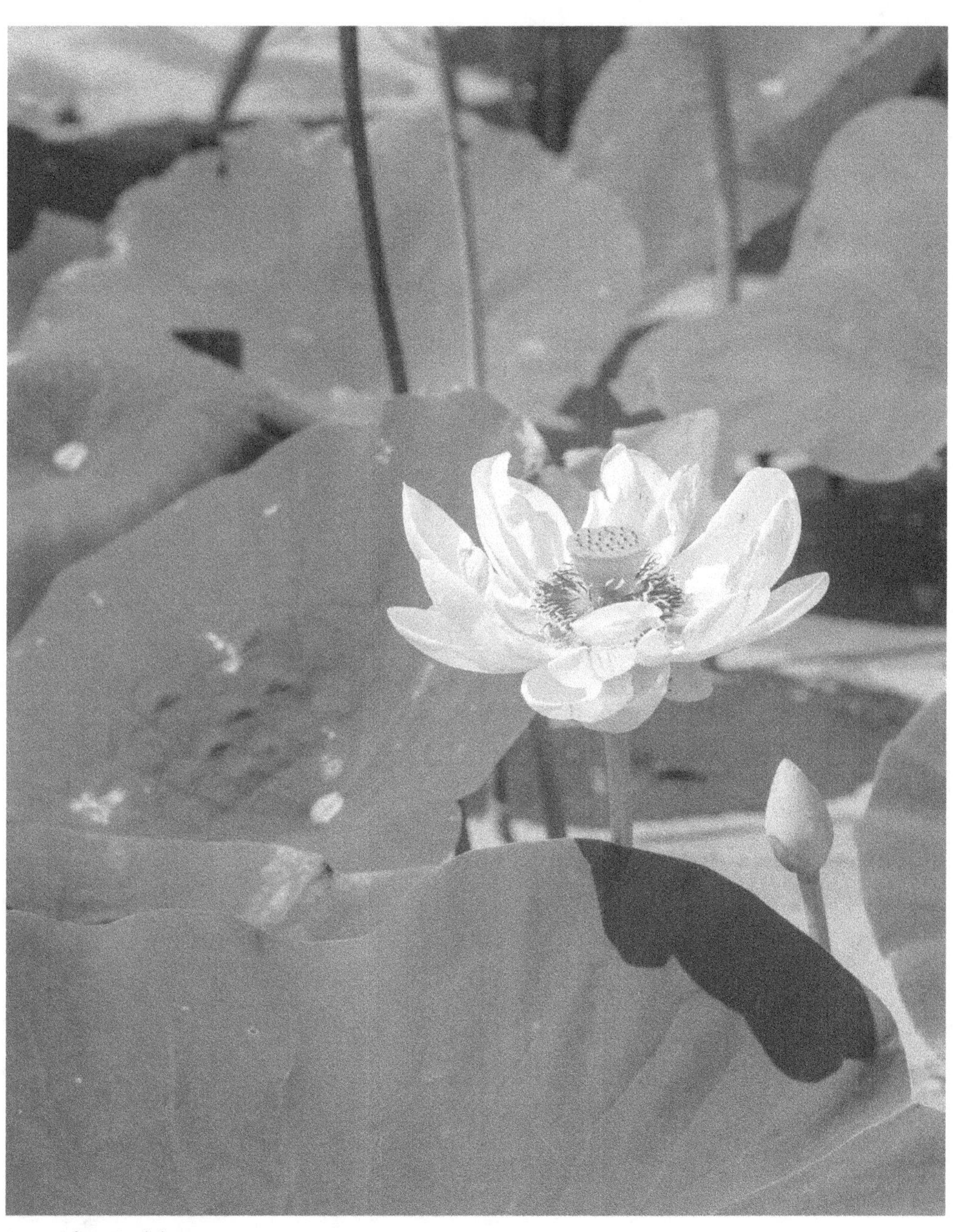

Jennifer Goldring
The Lotus Always Finds Its Way, 2020

www.ingramcontent.com/pod-product-compliance
Lightning Source LLC
LaVergne TN
LVHW020651100826
845148LV00012B/2432

* 9 7 9 8 2 1 8 2 9 2 2 0 1 *